WRITERS AND THEIR WORK

Isobel Armstrong
General Editor

WILLIAM GOLDING

WILLIAM GOLDING

Kevin McCarron

Second Edition

NORTHCOTE

BRITISH COUNCIL

ATLANTIC
PUBLISHERS & DISTRIBUTORS (P) LTD

This edition is published by

ATLANTIC
PUBLISHERS & DISTRIBUTORS (P) LTD
7/22, Ansari Road, Darya Ganj, New Delhi-110 002
Tel: 40775252, 23273880, 23275880, 23280451; Fax: +91-11-23285873
E-mail: orders@atlanticbooks.com; Web: www.atlanticbooks.com

By arrangement with
Northcote House Publishers Ltd
Horndon House, Horndon, Tavistock, Devon, PL19 9NQ,
United Kingdom. (T)+44(0)1822 810066; (F)+44(0)1822 810034
(E) northcote.house@virgin.net and (W) www.northcotehouse.co.uk
The *Writers and their Work* series is published in association with
the British Council.

Second edition 2006
First Indian Reprint 2010
First published in 1994 by Northcote House Publishers Ltd

ISBN 978-81-269-1321-3

For sale in the Indian sub-continent only. Not for export elsewhere.

British Library Cataloguing-in-Publication Data
A catalogue record for this book is available from the British Library

Typeset by PDQ Typesetting, Stoke-on-Trent
Printed in India at Nice Printing Press, A-33/3A, Site-IV,
Industrial Area, Sahibabad, Ghaziabad, U.P.

Contents

Acknowledgements

The author and the publishers are grateful to the following for permission to quote copyright material as follows:

Faber and Faber Limited (World excluding USA): *The Inheritors, Pincher Martin, Free Fall, The Spire, The Pyramid, The Scorpion God, The Hot Gates, A Moving Target, Darkness Visible, The Paper Men, Rites of Passage, Close Quarters, Fire Down Below, Lord of the Flies.* (World including USA): *The Brass Butterfly, An Egyptian Journal.*

In the USA. **Harcourt Brace & Company**: *The Inheritors, Pincher Martin, Free Fall, The Spire, The Pyramid, The Scorpion God, The Hot Gates.* **Farrar, Straus & Giroux, Inc.**: *A Moving Target, Darkness Visible, The Paper Men, Rites of Passage, Close Quarters, Fire Down Below,* **The Putnam Berkley Group Inc.**: *Lord of the Flies.*

Biographical Outline

1911	Born at St Columb Minor in Cornwall, 19 September.
1930	Attended Brasenose College, Oxford, to read Science.
1932	Changed over to Literature.
1934	*Poems* published.
1935	Graduated from Oxford.
1939	Married Ann Brookfield, and taught at Bishop Wordsworth's School in Salisbury.
1940-5	Joined the Royal Navy in 1940 and served until 1945.
1945	Returned to Bishop Wordsworth's School and taught English and Classics.
1954	*Lord of the Flies* published.
1955	Made a Fellow of the Royal Society of Literature.
1962	Left Bishop Wordsworth's School to concentrate on writing.
1966	Awarded CBE.
1980	Received Booker Prize for *Rites of Passage*.
1983	Awarded Nobel Prize for Literature.
1988	Knighted.
1993	Died at home in Truro, Cornwall on 19 June.
1995	*The Double Tongue* published.

1

Intertextuality and Evil

Always the truth is metaphorical.

('Fable')

William Gerald Golding was born at St Columb Minor, Cornwall, on 19 September 1911. He died on 19 June 1993 at his home in Truro, Cornwall. His father, Alec, was a schoolteacher and his mother, Mildred, was an enthusiastic supporter of the suffragette movement. Alec Golding taught at Marlborough Grammar School and William attended this school until he went to Brasenose College, Oxford, in 1930. He studied science for two years and then changed over to the study of English Literature. He graduated in 1935 and also studied for a Diploma in Education. While at Oxford he published his first book, a small volume of poems, which in later life he all but disowned. However, several of the poems share a thoughtful questioning of rational thought; a preoccupation that, as will be seen, is a constant feature of his subsequent fiction.

After Oxford, Golding worked as a teacher in the area of adult education, and also as a part-time actor, stage manager and producer; trades which are referred to in *Pincher Martin*. In 1939 he married Ann Brookfield, with whom he had two children and he became a teacher at Bishop Wordsworth's School, a grammar school in Salisbury. In December 1940 he joined the Royal Navy and served until the war ended in 1945. The war had a decisive impact on Golding as a man and as an artist. He served on mine sweepers, destroyers and cruisers, and eventually became a lieutenant, commanding his own rocket launcher. Although Golding is not a 'war novelist' in the conventional sense of the phrase, war provides the background to many of his novels: *Lord of the Flies*, *Pincher Martin*, *Free Fall*, *Darkness Visible* and *Rites of Passage*. The war forced Golding to query even more forcefully than he had done at Oxford the scientific, rationalistic, and ultimately optimistic picture of the world his father had offered him. In his essay, 'Fable', Golding writes of his experiences in the Second World War: 'I must say that anyone who moved through these years without understanding that man produces evil, as a bee produces honey, must have been blind or sick in the head.'

After the war Golding returned to Bishop Wordworth's School, where he taught English and Classics. While teaching he wrote several novels, all of which were rejected and which seem to have vanished forever. The book that was to make him a household name, *Lord of the Flies*, was itself rejected by twenty-one publishers, until Faber published it in 1954. *Lord of the Flies* was well received by the reviewers, and several very influential writers, including E. M. Forster, C. S. Lewis and T. S. Eliot, were very enthusiastic about the novel. It became a huge international success and has now been translated into twenty-six languages and sold millions of copies.

Throughout the late fifties and early sixties, however, Golding continued to teach at Bishop Wordsworth's School. During these years he published *The Inheritors* (1955), *Pincher Martin* (1956), his only play, *The Brass Butterfly* (1958), and *Free Fall* (1959). In 1962 he left teaching and devoted himself to writing. For many years he continued to live in Salisbury, but eventually moved to the more remote Truro in Cornwall. Golding was made a Fellow of the Royal Society of Literature in 1955 and was awarded the CBE in 1966. In 1980 he received the Booker Prize for *Rites of Passage*, and in 1983 he was awarded the Nobel Prize for Literature. In 1988 he was knighted and became Sir William Golding.

His interests were present in his writing to a considerable degree. He was a keen and adventurous sailor, an amateur archaeologist, and had a great love of classical Greek, which he taught himself to read – several critics have noted that Golding's harsh, austere novels share something of the spirit generated by Greek tragedy. Golding's war service, his knowledge of small boys, his love of sailing, are clearly of importance to any understanding of his work, but although we know a number of facts about Golding's life these facts can never, in themselves, explain the fiction. Critics can help, to some degree, but so too can reading as much of Golding's considerable body of work as possible.

William Golding's work was always slightly out of step with that of his fellow writers who were publishing novels in the early and middle 1950s. While novelists such as Kingsley Amis, John Wain, and Iris Murdoch seemed, initially at least, to be describing parochial worlds of considerable limitations, Golding was writing bold, visionary fables which claimed for themselves a universal applicability. *Lord of the Flies* is such a book. Golding's first novel is still his best-known work, and probably always will be, while *The Inheritors* is both his own favourite among his novels and the one with which readers most commonly experience difficulty. These two novels between them address issues such as rationalism, evil, evolution, and religion; themes which reappear throughout Golding's career. For this reason more space will be devoted to these novels than to any of the others, although everything Golding has published will be discussed, however briefly, in this short book.

Lord of the Flies is one of the best-known books of the post-war years. A group of young boys, the oldest of whom is 12 and the youngest 6, are marooned on a desert island, and almost immediately a battle for supremacy takes place among the principal characters. Violence and death follow. Golding's schoolboys are in a plane which has been shot down during what the reader assumes is a war set in the near future. Generically, therefore, *Lord of the Flies* can be seen as a dystopian (anti-Utopian) novel, linked with a number of important novels published this century: Yvgeny Zamyatin's *We*, Aldous Huxley's *Brave New World*, George Orwell's *Nineteen Eighty-Four*, Anthony Burgess's *A Clockwork Orange*, Margaret Atwood's *The Handmaid's Tale*, and a number of others.

Certainly, Golding's novel is as pessimistic as any of these dystopias. Although the boys begin by electing a leader, Ralph, and call frequent meetings, using a conch shell as a symbol of authority, their attempts at re-creating 'civilization' quickly founder. Jack Merridew, who is in charge of hunting, rapidly assumes dominance over the boys, exploiting their superstitious fears of 'the beast', and he eventually leaves Ralph's group, taking most of the other boys with him. When Simon, a visionary youth, realizes that 'the beast' is just a dead parachutist and attempts to communicate this knowledge to the other boys, Jack's 'tribe' ritualistically murder him. Piggy, the first of Golding's numerous Rationalist figures, is murdered by Jack's lieutenant, Roger, while he pathetically holds on to the conch, still believing in civilization. Ralph, now completely alone, is hunted like an animal by the other boys, who clearly intend to sacrifice him when they catch him. The forest is set on fire in order to smoke Ralph out and, just as he is about to be killed, an English ship sees the smoke and sends a rescue party.

The novel is usually read as Golding's commentary upon human evil, and almost certainly it would not have been written had Belsen and Auschwitz never existed, or indeed had Dresden never been bombed by the Allies, but it is also worth noting that Golding's early fiction is as much indebted to literature itself as it is to 'reality'. Contemporary literary critics use the term 'intertextuality' to designate the various relationships that a given text may have with another text, and *Lord of the Flies* is a 'rewriting' of R. M. Ballantyne's *The Coral Island* (1858), just as *The Inheritors* is a 'rewriting' of H. G. Wells's 'The Grisly Folk' (1921). All texts carry within them certain assumptions and values, and so when Golding 'rewrites' these earlier texts he is also criticizing these assumptions and values. While Golding's first novel is a grim rejoinder to Ballantyne's Victorian optimism, his second re-evaluates the slightly different type of optimism found in the work of H. G. Wells.

In 'Fable', Golding writes: 'It is worth looking for a moment at the great original of boys on an island. This is *The Coral Island*, published a century ago, at the height of Victorian smugness, ignorance and prosperity.' Ballantyne's book is optimistic in an imperialist, Victorian manner. Evil lies firmly outside the English schoolboys in this book and is made manifest by savage, black cannibals. In *Lord of the Flies* Golding has one of the boys say: 'After all, we're not savages. We're English; and the English are best at everything.' But throughout the novel, Golding overturns Ballantyne's optimistic portrait, which equates English with good and foreign with evil, and suggests that evil is more likely to reside within humanity, including the English, and that external evil is a projection of an inner evil. In doing this, Golding is offering a critique of Victorian Imperialism.

In *Lord of the Flies* Golding uses the same names for his central characters as Ballantyne does for his trio of brave, clean, young Englishmen, which assists the comparison and eventual subversion of the beliefs central to Ballantyne's book. Golding's characters are also used to portray sharply differing points of view on the nature of evil, and the means of placating this powerful force. For Piggy, there is no such thing as evil – it is just people behaving irrationally; for Jack, evil resides outside humanity and must be placated by various forms of sacrifice; and for Simon, evil expresses itself in the words of the Lord of the Flies: evil is inside humanity. Conversely, the depiction of evil in *The Coral Island* is strikingly simplistic, revolving about a specifically Christian/pagan dichotomy. Ballantyne offers a solution to the problem of evil at the end of *The Coral Island* that Golding has introduced at the beginning of his novel, and it is, significantly, no solution at all. *The Coral Island* insistently suggests that the cruelty and savagery of the pagans are due to their unfortunate ignorance of Christianity, and it is precisely this optimistic view that Golding seeks to subvert in *Lord of the Flies*.

Golding informs his readers immediately that the context of his characters' lives is specifically Christian: '"I ought to be chief," said Jack with simple arrogance, "because I'm chapter chorister and head boy."' The choir is a specifically religious institution and yet it is Jack and his hunters who become the most cruel and violent of all the boys on the island. In *Lord of the Flies*, therefore, we find an adumbration of the disturbing connection between religion, violence and blood sacrifice that Golding examines in close detail throughout the first phase of his career, and which is realized most powerfully in *The Spire*. As Golding's first novel moves us forward we constantly encounter this connection and must wonder if Jack and his choir become hunters and sacrificers of other human beings despite their obvious Christian origins, or because of them.

That *Lord of the Flies* does move us forward is something few readers would deny. It is as fine an adventure story as any published since the war, and yet Golding's ability to employ language which both provides narrative impetus and also evokes profounder, more theological, implications is demonstrated immediately: 'Taking their cue from the *innocent* Johnny, they sat down on the *fallen* palm tree and waited' (my emphasis). The novel is spare, deliberate in its intentions; and certainly Golding himself has little hesitation in referring to it as a 'fable'. *Lord of the Flies* is economical, so that the plane crash is not only a plausible device to isolate the boys, but is also essential as a commentary on the world outside the island. The novel is an examination not of the idiosyncratic nature of small boys, but of the essential nature of humanity itself, the heart of darkness. The island becomes a microcosm of the adult world, which is also destroying itself. The grim account of propitiation and murder on the island, Golding suggests, is re-enacted in the greater world continuously, and this interaction between the two worlds is powerfully dramatized in Golding's use of the dead parachutist.

Bewildered and frightened, the children yearn for a sign from the adult world, but the sign that is sent is fraught with meaning, possessing a symbolic power which persists throughout the novel. The dead parachutist is himself a scapegoat, a victim of the war which rages as the adults' madness increases on a scale microcosmically reflected by the boys on the island. In his essay 'Crabbed Youth and Age', Golding refers to the millions of young men who were slaughtered during the First World War as 'the pure and blameless, the eternally sacrificed'. The dead parachutist, too, is invested with some of this eternal, mythic quality, and yet in this most economical of novels he also gives the children the chance to externalize their apprehension of evil. It is his baleful, rotting presence which allows them to ignore Simon's pregnant suggestion: 'What I mean is ... maybe it's only us.'

Writing on the ostensibly innocuous subject of fairy stories, Golding writes in another of his essays, 'Custodians of the Real': 'Inside a fairy tale or out of it, a severed head is a powerful affair.' This comment is dramatized in *Lord of the Flies* when the hunters place the severed head of a pig in the clearing. To the hunters, this offering is one of propitiation; they have projected evil outside themselves. But Simon realizes that the severed head is an ineradicable part of humanity: 'At last Simon gave up and looked back; saw the white teeth and dim eyes, the blood – and his gaze was held by that ancient, inescapable recognition.' When Simon attempts to communicate his knowledge that the parachutist is a pathetic victim of a larger war and that evil is internal, he is torn to pieces by Jack's tribe. Similarly, when Piggy tries to reason with the boys he is killed. Golding constructs a complex metaphorical system around Piggy; the conch shell and his glasses being paramount. For Piggy, who has intelligence, but no intuitive powers, the conch *is* order, and he fails to realize that the conch in itself is nothing, a literally hollow shell, unless the others agree on its symbolic powers. When Jack's tribe steal his glasses to make fire and Piggy stands among them, blind, fat, and trembling, his words – almost his last – are genuinely tragic in their uncomprehending innocence: 'I tell you, I got the conch.'

Completely alone, as Lok will be at the end of *The Inheritors*, Ralph runs for his life. He is crying for mercy, on the point of being murdered, when a naval officer appears to save him. Golding himself has described the ending as a 'gimmick' but, strictly speaking, it is a shift in perspective; a device which he also uses at the end of *The Inheritors* and *Pincher Martin*. As a technique, it is clearly indebted to the Greek concept of the *deus ex machina*, a supernatural intervention, and in *Lord of the Flies* the effect of this shift in perspective is considerable. Most importantly it reminds us that the characters we have been seeing as hunters and killers are only children, while the officer's patronizing air alerts us to the fact that precisely the same horrors are being re-enacted in the adult world. Ralph is blinded by tears; his bitter understanding of the evil that resides within humanity both anticipates what is to be a consistent theme of Golding's in the novels which follow, and also provides a darkly ironic counterpoint to the officer's helpful comment: 'I know. Jolly good show. Like The Coral Island.' Golding's island is a hundred years and two world wars away from the blithe and callous optimism of Ballantyne, and this prepares us for the very much greater irony contained both in the epigraph to Golding's second novel, and in its very title, *The Inheritors*.

The plot of *The Inheritors* is as straightforward as that of *Lord of the Flies*, and indeed is similar to it: a small group of Neanderthalers is systematically killed by a larger and more powerful group of 'New Men', *Homo sapiens*. The difficulty some readers experience with *The Inheritors* is generally traceable to the novel's point of view. The nature of perception, the way in which we see, is central to *The Inheritors* and remains a constant issue throughout all Golding's fiction. The novel is far more easily understood once we accept that we are observing the Neanderthalers' primitive and violent world through eyes that cannot comprehend what they are seeing. In *The Inheritors*, Golding makes us see through a perspective so brutally limited and simple that the novel appears, perhaps paradoxically, difficult and complex.

In *The Inheritors*, so much of the narrative is refracted through the uncomprehending perceptions of Lok that it becomes impossible to separate Golding's manipulation of an extraordinarily limited perspective from the novel's thematic structure. In his essay 'An Affection For Cathedrals', Golding himself says of such issues: 'For what is a work of art? Is it the form or the substance? "Both", we feel, when we think about it at all, "but if we must choose, give us the substance."' *The Inheritors* does not offer its reader this choice; the form and the substance are inextricably connected. The passage in which Lok first directly confronts one of the New Men might serve as an example of the way in which theme and perspective are inseparable in this novel. The 'point of view' is Lok's as it is throughout most of the novel, and he watches with fascination as the New Man across the river plays with a stick:

> The stick began to grow shorter at both ends. Then it shot out to full length again. 'Clop!'
>
> His ears twitched and he turned to the tree. By his face there had grown a twig: a twig that smelt of other, and of goose, and of the bitter berries that Lok's stomach told him he must not eat.

Once the reader has realized the limitations of Lok's perceptions, this incident is easily understood. Lok knows nothing of human violence and has no real fear of it. The reader, however, sees quite clearly that the 'stick' is a bow, and that the reason it gets 'shorter at both ends' is because the New Man is about to fire it at him. The arrow hits a nearby tree ('Clop!') and Lok believes that 'the tree had grown a twig'. Incapable of understanding the act of violence just directed at him, Lok sees the arrow as something natural, something organic. Similarly, while Lok remains innocent of the implications of the 'bitter berries', the reader understands that the arrow is poisoned.

Here, and indeed throughout the novel, Golding is doing something remarkable. Normally when we read fiction we are pleased at our ability to comprehend; we pat ourselves on the back for having worked out where Pip's money comes from in Dickens's *Great Expectations*, or for understanding that *Lord of the Flies* is a novel about the ways humans project evil. But *The Inheritors* does not offer us this sense of superiority over the text. This is not because the novel is too complex to understand, far from it, but that, forced to view shocking events – which we understand – through uncomprehending eyes, we are manipulated into a position of complicity with guilt, and our knowledge does not flatter us, it condemns us. Although we are inclined to sympathize with Lok's people, Golding's technique forces us to realize that we belong with the New Men; we are the Inheritors. The novel also calls into question precisely what it is we have inherited, and suggests that principal among our legacies is guilt.

This is an issue which is central to both *Pincher Martin* and *Free Fall*, and also to his essay 'Digging for Pictures'. While digging as an amateur archaeologist, Golding came across the remains of an old woman, and he writes of his sensations as she was covered over again with earth:

> There is a sense in which I share the guilt buried beneath the runway, a sense in which my imagination has locked me to them. I share in what was at the least a callous act – in what at the worst may very well have been a prehistoric murder.

From the novel's beginning, the New Men, us, are associated with disruption, violence and death. The title seems to contain a sombre pun on 'Blessed are the meek: for they shall inherit the earth' (Matthew 5: 5), as throughout the course of this novel we realize that here the meek do not 'inherit' the earth, rather we, *Homo sapiens*, do – and the meek are completely destroyed.

In his *Outline of History*, (London, 1951), from which Golding takes the epigraph to his novel, H. G. Wells writes: 'as the Fourth Glacial Age softened towards more temperate conditions, a different human type came upon the European scene, and it would seem exterminated *Homo Neanderthalis*' (p. 85). The equanimity of Wells's tone here is complemented by the narrative voice of his short story 'The Grisly Folk'. In this story, Wells describes the adventures of a group of our remote ancestors, a tribe of hunter-gatherers whom Wells refers to throughout as the 'true men'. This tribe have one of their children stolen by 'the grisly folk', a tribe which Wells also refers to as the 'pre-men', and whom he persistently reduces to animal or 'thing' status. In 'The Grisly Folk', the 'true men' have one of their children abducted by the 'pre-men'. Golding inverts Wells's plot, and in *The Inheritors* it is the 'true men' who do the kidnapping, and it is they who are the cannibals.

Perhaps not surprisingly, the two perspectives suggested by the title and the epigraph: the religious and the anthropological, dominate critical assessments of *The Inheritors*. The novel is invariably read as an evolutionary fable, while some critics argue that it also needs to be read as a religious allegory. However, both *Lord of the Flies* and *The Inheritors* 'rewrite' earlier texts and it is not only the plots of the earlier works which are being re-examined, but so too are the attitudes which underlie both texts. Wells's 'The Grisly Folk' is optimistic in an evolutionary, Darwinian sense and his story is predicated upon the belief that humanity has progressed in every possible way since the beginning of time, and will continue to do so. The phrase he uses to describe the Neanderthalers, 'the pre-men', makes this quite clear; they are not yet 'true men', they are not sufficiently evolved to deserve respect or consideration.

Colonialism can also be seen as an issue in *The Inheritors;* one that is linked to evolutionary theories. If one is at the top of the evolutionary ladder, then one has no moral obligation to respect the rights, or even the lives, of those who have yet to reach this plateau. Instead, there is a moral duty to impose one's superior values on all those people who remain in a state of unenlightened savagery, and if they remain obdurate then it is permissible to kill them. A large number of British novelists have written about Colonialism and Imperialistic conflict: Rudyard Kipling, George Orwell, Winifred Holtby, Joyce Cary, Paul Scott, and, with *The Inheritors,* perhaps William Golding could be added to that list. A reading of the novel which sees Lok's people as the colonized and the New Men as the colonizers does not displace other readings, but may be seen as an indication of the ways in which fabular constructions, in particular, are amenable to a variety of approaches.

One of Golding's principal interests in his early fiction is examining the ways in which humanity projects its internal evil onto something external. It is this issue of 'projection' which accounts for the stress Golding lays in these early novels upon the scapegoat, human sacrifice, and, in *The Inheritor*s, upon cannibalism. The narrator of 'The Grisly Folk' is emphatic that it would be the Neanderthalers who were cannibals, but in *The Inheritors,* it is Liku who is eaten by the New Men, the Inheritors, us. Golding's novel suggests that it is Wells's 'true men' who are the cannibals, and who, in their fear, have projected their own evil impulses onto the gentler tribe, thereby justifying their extermination. If Colonialism is viewed as a form of absorbing, or 'devouring', the colonized country, then cannibalism will be seen as one of its most potent metaphors. The irony that runs throughout the novel, of course, is that Lok's people are no threat at all; not only are they not cannibals, they are only carnivorous in exceptional circumstances. The New Men assume Lok's tribe are cannibals only because, as colonizers, they are projecting their own desires and appetites for complete absorption onto a conquered people, the colonized.

The acts of sacrifice and propitiation which are so important in *Lord of the Flies* are equally important in *The Inheritors,* and for many of the same reasons. They are a way of projecting, and then attempting to appease, an evil which is really internal. Lok and Fa, for example, find 'presents' which have been left for them by the New Men. These gifts are an act of propitiation similar to the one which is made in *Lord of the Flies* when Jack's hunters leave out their gift for 'the beast'. From this perspective, Lok and Fa have been turned into the 'grisly folk', the 'beast'. To the New Men they are devils and must be placated, even to the extent of offering Tanakil as a blood sacrifice. *The Inheritors* is a novel as deeply concerned as its predecessor with humanity's persistent attempt to locate evil outside itself, and then to offer it blood, in the doomed hope that 'then it will leave us alone maybe'.

While the religion of the New Men is patriarchal and is as inevitably aggressive as its practitioners, the religion of Golding's Neanderthalers is strikingly matriarchal. Throughout the novel, and particularly in its opening chapters, Golding presents us with the innocent life of the People. Their lives are hard and mundane and brutal, but we still see their sense of tribal communion, their gentleness, their physicality and love of play, and their worship of a female deity who abhors bloodshed. Oa is fecund and protective; she inspires joy, not fear. Oa is clearly the opposite of the rutting, bellowing Stag God of the New Men, and yet the reader is forced to accept that any culture based upon Christianity has more in common with this violent being than it does with the gentle Oa. Another clear distinction is drawn when we see that among the People it is the women who control the tribe's religious life. When Lok follows the women into the cave of ice where Oa is worshipped, and which is to melt while Lok dies alone in a poignantly symbolic episode near the end of the novel, he is terrified by the sense of religious power he feels, and Fa is forced to comfort him by saying 'It is too much Oa for a man.' The life-affirming vision of the People embodies a set of values which cannot comprehend blood sacrifice, something which is, as is revealed while Lok and Fa are in the tree, central to the religion of the New Men.

The New Men murder any of the People they encounter, and then abduct Liku and the 'new one'; a reversal, of course, of Wells's 'The Grisly Folk'. Lok and the woman, Fa, follow the New Men to their camp and observe their actions from the vantage point of a dead tree, which itself provides a 'realistic' theological symbol. As the events progress they remain incomprehensible to Lok, but the reader, despite being seriously blinkered by Lok's limited perspective, manages to work out what the New Men are doing, if not, at this point, the full implications of these actions. Throughout the chapters in which Lok and Fa gaze down on the clearing, we see, through Lok's eyes, the New Men's rutting, masculine Stag God, and the violent, drunken, sexually orgiastic behaviour – and a mute comparison between the two tribes underlies the whole sequence of events. Golding employs his technique of making us see only that which Lok can see so effectively that many readers may only discover what has happened to Liku at the same moment of revelation as Lok: 'Out of the churned-up earth the right forepaw picked a small, white bone.' The New Men have killed Liku and eaten her. But precisely because Lok is not perceptive enough to realize this, he involves Fa, who does know, in a hopeless attempt to rescue her. As they run from the clearing, Fa is hit by a rock and falls into the river. She manages to clutch onto a tree but, while Lok runs helplessly along the bank, the current picks up speed. 'The tree hung for a while with the head facing upstream. Slowly the root end sank and the head rose. Then it slid forward soundlessly and dropped over the fall.' This is another instance in which the realistic and the symbolic are interwoven. The very movement of the tree – 'the root end sank and the head rose' – reflects the movement of the narrative as a whole: the People have sunk into oblivion and the New Men have 'risen'.

It is at this point in the novel that Golding gives us, for the first time a description of Lok:

> It was a strange creature, smallish, and bowed. The legs and thighs were bent and there was a whole thatch of curls on the outside of the legs and arms. The back was high, and covered over the shoulders with curly hair. Its feet and hands were broad, and flat, the great toe projecting inwards to grip. The square hands swung down to the knees.

This description has clearly been delayed so that the reader is not prejudiced by Lok's appearance. Here again, technique and themes are inseparable. Although it is now quite clear that Lok does indeed look like one of Wells's 'Grisly Folk', we have seen virtually every incident within the novel through his eyes. Consequently, we have a sympathy for him that will not be destroyed by this description of his physical appearance. This sympathy is so strong that the account of Lok's final moments of life is among the most poignant episodes in contemporary fiction.

Lok is alone in a way one of the New Men could not begin to understand, and it may be to emphasize this that Golding does not have him killed in the same way as the others. Lok is totally different from characters like Daniel Defoe's Robinson Crusoe or Golding's own Christopher Martin, men who endure the most extreme hardships and solitude rather than die. Lok has no life outside his People; his is an identity which only has meaning within a collective, tribal framework. The moment when Lok realizes he is completely alone and begins to cry is almost uncomfortably moving. Lok is alone in a way that we can only begin to comprehend, and this is the reason that he simply lies down to die. He tries to climb into Mal's grave, one of the People to the end, but he lacks the physical strength. The narrator's dispassionate tone adds immeasurably to the power of this episode, and the more Lok is referred to as 'it', the more we see him as 'he', and the more moving the scene becomes. This suggestion of complicity in his own death, this awesome loneliness of Lok, anticipates Parson Colley and his lonely, self-willed death in *Rites of Passage* (1980).

This phrase 'rites of passage' could serve as a subtitle for the last chapter of *The Inheritors*, which now, in the closing pages, switches perspectives in exactly the same way as *Lord of the Flies* did at the same point within its narrative. This time, the shift in perspective effectively prevents us from reading the novel as a simple conflict between good (the People) and bad (the New Men). Although it is made quite clear throughout the novel that the People were unsuited to the demands of a more complex age, this important point may have been overshadowed by the pathos of Lok's death. However, it is important that we remember Mal's description of the People's past and acknowledge that while they had once been a large tribe, flourishing in a congenial environment, they were obviously too passive and in any case lacked the intelligence to undertake the rigours of adaptation. When the novel begins, this once numerous tribe are reduced to eight members, and are totally at the mercy of the harsh new seasons. Even had the New Men not arrived, Lok's people could not have survived; they were doomed to extinction by the lack of those qualities which enable the New Men to control their environment.

While the destruction of the People may sadden us, this final chapter ensures we do not make the sentimental mistake of blaming the New Men. In the beginning of the novel, Mal recounted the history of his people, and in this final chapter we learn the history of the New Men and, perhaps against all expectations, we begin to sympathize with them as well. We learn their real names, not the ones Lok gave them, and the polysyllabic nature of them (Marlan, Tuami) is a way of emphasizing how much more complex they are than Lok's tribe. Tuami is complex enough to recognize that the price of survival is the knowledge of guilt: 'What else could we have done?' The very cry of despair that Tuami utters suggests the growth of a new, more refined consciousness, one that could not have come into existence without the knowledge of evil and guilt. So too does his recognition that his knife can be used for the act of creation, as well as that of destruction. Similarly, the 'new one's' actual presence suggests the possibility of a reconciliation between innocence and guilt.

Such readings, however, may place too great a faith in the potential of both the artist, Tuami, and in art in general, while ignoring the insidious figure of Marlan. Tuami has a powerful vision; he understands that it is *only* through the existence of evil that good may come. Marlan lacks Tuami's vision; he is unable to see that he is projecting his own inner evil onto the outside world – but it is significant that Marlan has the final word: 'They live in darkness under the trees.'

While both *Lord of the Flies* and *The Inheritors* consider the notion of projection on a grand scale, and assess its implications for humanity and for history, Golding's third novel reduces the scale of its concern and focuses on one unique individual, Christopher Martin, known as Pincher Martin.

Like its immediate predecessors, although not as obviously, *Pincher Martin* is indebted to earlier literary sources. Again, the plot is extremely simple; the difficulty readers often experience with it is, as with *The Inheritors*, due to the complex form of expression. During World War II, Christopher Martin, a lieutenant in the navy, is thrown from the bridge of his ship when it is hit by a torpedo, and the novel opens with him struggling in the water. The novel describes him finding a small rock in the middle of the ocean and then recounts, in extraordinary detail, his grim struggle for survival on this rock. The final chapter offers us, as did the two earlier novels, a shift in perspective, but this is the most dramatic of them all, because at this point in *Pincher Martin* we discover that the protagonist has been dead since the opening pages of the novel. (In

America the novel was originally published under the title *The Two Deaths of Christopher Martin*.) The ending has provoked considerable hostile criticism over the years, but *Pincher Martin* shares some of the characteristics of the detective story as well as of the survival narrative, and the author leaves a number of clues scattered throughout the novel which, cumulatively, reveal the true state of affairs. At one point in the novel Martin says to himself: 'Strange that bristles go on growing even when the rest of you is –'. The reader finishes the sentence, as Martin cannot utter the word 'dead'; to do so would mean acknowledging the falsity of his creation and would condemn him to death.

In its central conceit Golding's novel is reminiscent of Ambrose Bierce's short story 'An Occurrence at Owl Creek Bridge', a story which tells the reader only at the very end that the central character has been dead from the opening lines. *Pincher Martin* may also be 'rewriting' a novel by Henry Dorling (who wrote under the name of Taffrail), published in 1916, and called *Pincher Martin, OD*. Just like Golding's character, Taffrail's Pincher is thrown into the sea when his ship is torpedoed, but unlike Taffrail's character Golding's Pincher does not surrender himself to the sea and to death; he is too self-obsessed to die. *Pincher Martin* investigates a greed so intense, a pride so enormous, that death becomes unthinkable. As Martin struggles in the sea we are told his thoughts:

> I won't die.
> I can't die.
> Not me.
> Precious.

Although *Pincher Martin* is the first of Golding's novels to take place in the contemporary world, it is also a book set on an island, and one that is concerned with survival and isolation, those perennial Golding themes. Similarly, just as the boys in *Lord of the Flies* project their fears and horrors onto 'the beast', and the New People in *The Inheritors* turn the gentle Neanderthalers into demons, so Martin in this novel turns an aching tooth in his own mouth into an island in the middle of the ocean, and creates from his egotistical and perverse refusal to die a heroic struggle for survival.

Again, like its predecessors, *Pincher Martin* is a deeply moral fable, as it seems that Martin's punishment is directly proportionate to the life he had led. Our knowledge of his previous life is revealed in a series of flashbacks and one of the novel's dominant structural devices is this alternation between past and present; between the world and the rock. As the novel progresses our admiration for Martin's epic fight for life is slowly undermined by our increasing knowledge of his viciousness and greed. The flashbacks also introduce us to Mary, one of the few women ever to refuse him, and Nat, Martin's only friend, who marries her. It is his attempt to murder Nat that causes him to fall into the ocean, which in turn leads to his creation of the rock and his own creation of himself as tragic hero. The language of drama permeates the novel – the opening reference to a stage is succeeded by memories of Martin's career as an actor and, ultimately, by his attempts to play the great tragic roles. As the illusory nature of his survival becomes inexorably more apparent to Martin, he even turns to the great figures of myth to keep reality from intruding, re-creating himself as Ajax and Prometheus. Unable to maintain this fantasy, Martin shows characteristic cunning in deciding that he is mad, preferring this to death. It is significant, however, that while he adopts the role of Lear he misquotes, underlining his inability to play the part. Remorselessly, Martin is made to see the truth – he is not a king, transformed by suffering into a tragic figure, but a dead man who refuses to die.

Pincher Martin parodies the Genesis myth of creation and for six days and six nights Martin creates his world: the rock, the sea, the sky, night, day, the seaweed, the gulls, and the shell fish. He also 'names' his world, giving parts of the rock names from his old world: The Red Lion, Prospect Cliff ... Finally, on the sixth day, it seems that he creates God and the curtain comes down on Christopher Martin. The God he creates is in his own image, wearing an oilskin and seaboots, and it says to him 'Have you had enough, Christopher?' But Martin refuses to admit he has had enough, and screams defiance to the end. Finally he is reduced to a pair of claws (pincers), and is annihilated by the 'black lightning' which he remembers from his conversations with Nat and which is the only conception of an afterlife he possesses.

Although the parallels with Genesis might prompt the reader to assume that the figure who speaks to Martin is God, it is also possible that this is the voice of the author. As Martin begins to disintegrate in the face of the black lightning, references which could clearly refer to the act of writing begin to appear: 'The sea stopped moving, froze, became paper, painted paper that was torn by a black line. The rock was painted on the same paper.' Just as it is possible to read *The Inheritors* as a novel about post-colonialism, rather than as an evolutionary fable, so too *Pincher Martin* can be read as a metafictional novel, a text that openly comments on its own fictional status, rather than as a purely theological fable.

There are few novels which cannot be reread profitably, but to reread *Pincher Martin* with the knowledge that the protagonist is actually dead is to encounter a radically different book. The densely textured and graphically detailed descriptions of the rock and physical landscape which, on a first reading, persuaded us of the realism of Martin's plight, are now seen as deeply ironic. What the reader now recognizes is the appalling strain Martin experiences in maintaining the fantasy that the rock is real, a demand which clearly has an analogue with the creative process, and perhaps not only with writing but also with reading. Golding's interest in the process of creation itself, a concern which marks him as a contemporary writer, is further developed in his use of the painter Samuel Mountjoy, the protagonist of his next novel, *Free Fall.*

Free Fall has much in common with its predecessors, particularly with *Pincher Martin,* but it is also significantly different from the earlier three novels. For the first time Golding uses a first person narrator, and for the first time the world that this narrator describes is a recognizably modern world; one with a social dimension. While previously Golding had been interested in isolation, in depicting groups and individuals struggling for survival: in the future, in the past, and even in a world of his character's own making, now he portrays an individual in the contemporary world. Perhaps somewhat paradoxically then, many readers experience difficulty with *Free Fall* and it is generally seen as one of Golding's most 'difficult' novels. However, as with its predecessors, the difficulties lie less with the tale itself than with the telling of it.

Generically, *Free Fall* can be read as a Künstlerroman, a German word meaning 'artist novel', which is used to describe any work in which the central character is an artist of any kind. Perhaps the most famous modern example of the genre is James Joyce's *A Portrait of the Artist as a Young Man,* but there are a number of novels which, like *Free Fall,* feature painters as protagonists, including Joyce Cary's *The Horse's Mouth* and Patrick White's *The Vivisector.* In *Free Fall,* Golding uses Mountjoy's profession as an artist to comment on the general nature of artistic production. As an artist, Mountjoy selects and arranges his materials in order to create a pattern; something recognizable. This is what Mountjoy hopes to find as he re-examines his life – a pattern which will give meaning to his existence.

The chronological structure of *Free Fall* is inseparable from the novel's central concerns. In the opening pages Mountjoy writes:

> For time is not to be laid out endlessly like a row of bricks. That straight line from the first hiccup to the last gasp is a dead thing. Time is two modes. The one is an effortless perception native to us as water to the mackerel. The other is a memory, a sense of shuffle fold and coil, of that day nearer than that because more important ...

This conflict between dual perspectives is anticipated in the novel's title. The phrase 'free fall' suggests an object obeying the law of gravity and falling through space, but it also has religious connotations, suggesting the theological fall of humanity and it is possible that the title has been taken from Milton's epic poem *Paradise Lost* ('Sufficient to have stood I But free to fall').

The protagonist's name is also one that sets up dualities. 'Samuel' is the name of an Old Testament prophet, while 'Mountjoy' clearly possesses sexual connotations. This tension between the religious and the carnal, the spirit and the flesh, provides the central dynamic of *Free Fall*. These two totally different perceptions of life are personified in the characters of Mountjoy's schoolteachers, Nick Shales and Rowena Pringle. Shales is a scientist, a rationalist; while Pringle teaches Scripture, and tells the children of a world in which a bush can catch fire and yet be unconsumed by the flames. Throughout the novel, Mountjoy tries to find a way to reconcile these two visions, to find a bridge between the two worlds, and yet at the novel's conclusion he notes that Shales's world is real and so is Pringle's: 'There is no bridge.'

Like his previous novels, Golding's fourth book is indebted to an earlier literary source. *Free Fall* is a parody of Dante's *La Vita Nuova (The Poems of Youth)* (*c.* 1290), a collection of thirty-one lyrical poems celebrating the beauty and virtue of Dante's Beatrice (probably Beatrice dei Portinari, who married the Florentine banker Simone dei Bardi and died in 1290 at the age of 24). Dante's poem is interspersed with the poet's comments, in prose, which evaluate the development of his emotions, and which also analyse the poems themselves. There are a number of occasions where *Free Fall* is clearly and deliberately invoking *La Vita Nuova*. Dante unexpectedly sees Beatrice in a Florentine street accompanied by two other women; Mountjoy arranges events so that he can 'accidentally' run into his Beatrice as she leaves the training college accompanied by two other girls. Dante writes a poem to Beatrice to explain his feelings; Mountjoy writes a passionate letter to his Beatrice. Dante's feelings for Beatrice shift from despair to devotion as he walks by a stream in the country. Mountjoy similarly walks past a stream and his feelings of devotion change into compelling physical desire.

Golding's use of *La Vita Nuova* signals a shift in his practice up to this point. The earlier novels had incorporated literary analogues as a way of demonstrating the partiality, or even incorrectness, of the beliefs central to these texts, but in *Free Fall* Dante's poem is used to suggest that Mountjoy's desire for Beatrice Ifor is inferior to Dante's devotion to his Beatrice. Here, the views central to the earlier literary model are seen to be superior. Mountjoy is only interested in sex with his Beatrice (her surname 'I-for' underlines her object status for him) and, as a result, he deliberately chooses to sacrifice 'everything' so that he can possess her. The novel describes Mountjoy's attempt to locate the specific moment in his life when he lost his freedom, and to that extent *Free Fall* can also be seen as a 'quest narrative': 'How did I lose my freedom? I must go back and tell the story over.' The specific 'moment' for Mountjoy is almost certainly the moment in the woods, the parodic re-enactment of Dante's sublime vision, when Mountjoy asks himself a question and then answers it:

> What will you sacrifice?
> 'Everything.'

Several critics have suggested that the Dantean analogue only operates during those chapters which feature Beatrice Ifor, but it should be noted that through its use of a prose commentary *La Vita Nuova* is as much a book about the act of writing poetry as it is about Dante's devotion to Beatrice. Similarly, although Samuel Mountjoy is a painter, *Free Fall* is a first person narrative; one which is itself very much concerned with the act of writing. It is actually writing, rather than painting, which can be seen as the primary activity within the novel and, at the very beginning of the book, Golding draws attention to both the artificial and the commercial nature of reading and writing: 'And who are you anyway? Are you on the inside, have you a proof-copy? Am I a job to do? Do I exasperate you by translating incoherence into incoherence?' The way in which Mountjoy chooses to tell his story raises interesting questions about the artist's ability actually to portray 'reality', an issue Golding returns to in *Rites of Passage* and *The Paper Men*.

Free Fall adopts and then transforms the use of flashbacks used in *Pincher Martin*. While the earlier novel incorporated flashbacks into what was essentially a tightly organized linear narrative, *Free Fall* is structured as one chronologically disrupted flashback. Although this structure causes difficulties for some readers, it is by no means 'wilfully obscure', as one reviewer claimed when the book was first published. The chronology of the novel is based upon Mountjoy's memory, rather than on any objective or omniscient description of the sequence of events, and Mountjoy simply remembers events in the order of their importance to him. The novel can be divided into seven sections, each one of which contains images from the past. The first three chapters describe Mountjoy's childhood. The next three deal with his relationship with Beatrice, his association with the Communist Party, his apprenticeship as an artist, and his love for Taffy. Chapters seven, eight, and nine describe Mountjoy's experience in a German prisoner of war camp, and also contain a flashback to childhood. The next three chapters shift from a transcendent moment in the prison yard back to an account of Mountjoy's school encounters with Rowena Pringle and Nick Shales. In chapter twelve, Mountjoy chooses the flesh over the spirit when he says he will sacrifice 'everything' for Beatrice. The penultimate chapter shows Beatrice in an insane asylum, possibly indicating that someone else has paid Mountjoy's price. The final chapter returns us to the prison camp and sets up yet another of Golding's shifts in perspective; one that this time returns the reader, and the writer, to the beginning of the novel.

Several critics have suggested that this inability of Mountjoy's to find the bridge between the two worlds is equally a failure of the novel. However, this view seems to indicate that a successful novel must be 'closed', that is, must offer the reader a sense of resolution or completion. Mountjoy's failure is not Golding's. If the consistent intertextual relationship with Dante's *La Vita Nuova* is accepted, *Free Fall* can be seen as a book which is concerned not only with the attempt to find the truth, but also with the desire to communicate this truth. Early in the book, Mountjoy notes: 'To communicate is our passion and our despair.' Like Dante's poem, *Free Fall* ceaselessly investigates the ways in which we select the material we wish to communicate, and the nature of the language we use for this communication.

Golding's fifth novel, *The Spire,* is also structured around the act of communication – in this case a vision and a command from God. Like *Free Fall, The Spire* is an investigation of the two differing worlds of the spirit and the flesh but, unlike the earlier novel, *The Spire* moves towards an emphatic resolution; one which is clearly, though not unequivocally, tragic. When *The Spire* was published in 1964 a number of reviewers were hostile to the book, and complained that it was even more densely written than *Free Fall* and even more difficult to understand; a view that over the years large numbers of readers have echoed. However, *The Spire* is like all of Golding's early fiction in that a simple story is told in a complicated manner. In *The Spire,* as in *The Inheritors,* the complication can be seen in the narrative perspective. The novel has an omniscient narrator, but virtually every event within it is seen through Jocelin's eyes. This creates a perspective which is both uneasily ambivalent and brutally circumscribed, and this latter quality is paralleled in the claustrophobic, fourteenth-century setting of the novel. Similarly, the continuous blurring of the two narrative perspectives parallels the movement of the story toward the reconciliation of two worlds; an event most spectacularly realized in Jocelin's death-bed epiphany.

The chronology of *The Spire* is uncomplicated, covering two years in what is, essentially, a linear narrative. The story line of the novel is also quite straightforward. Jocelin, Dean of Barchester Cathedral, believes that he has been chosen by God to build a 400-foot-high spire on top of the cathedral. It quickly becomes apparent that the foundations under the cathedral will not support such a weight, and yet, against all sound practical advice, Jocelin persists with his dream. During the course of the novel the workmen murder Pangall, a deformed cathedral factotum, and Roger Mason, the builder, has an adulterous relationship with Pangall's wife, Goody, who later dies in childbirth. Jocelin eventually realizes that Pangall has been sacrificed in an attempt to appease the dark powers which the workmen worship, and he also realizes that he had encouraged the adulterous relationship in a successful attempt to keep Mason working on the spire. Revelation succeeds revelation and Jocelin also discovers that his own elevation to a deanship was due to the whim of a relative who was the king's mistress. The novel ends with all the principal characters dead or dying, but the spire, against all logic, still stands. Structurally, the novel can be seen to consist of two sections: the first section (chapters one to ten) describes the building of the spire, and the second section (chapters ten to twelve) evaluates this achievement.

After the contemporary social realism of *Free Fall*, *The Spire* marks a clear return to the territory of primitive isolation which had characterized Golding's fiction up to that point, but his fifth novel is also unlike any of its predecessors in one significant way. *The Spire* is the first of his books to use no literary analogue, although some critics have argued, not too convincingly, that Ibsen's play *The Master Builder* lies behind the novel. For the first time in Golding's work, the narrative seems to be based on historical facts rather than on earlier fiction. Golding lived in Salisbury for many years and *The Spire* is based on the actual building of the spire at Salisbury Cathedral in the fourteenth century. The names of his two principal characters, Jocelin and Roger, are those of two early bishops whose bodies are buried in the cathedral. The architectural details also coincide: Golding's spire is 400 feet high, Salisbury's is 404, the highest in England.

The Inheritors developed several central concerns of *Lord of the Flies*, and *The Spire* expands upon many issues raised in *The Inheritors*. Perhaps the most fully resolved of these similarities is to be found in the concept of 'cost', and in the title essay of *A Moving Target* Golding says of *The Spire*: 'The book is about the human cost of building the spire.' As *The Spire* progresses we witness the appalling personal price Jocelin is prepared to pay, and the price he inflicts upon the innocent. In *The Inheritors*, too, we were made aware of cost – of the awesome price the New Men had to pay in order to surmount their origins. One of Golding's most persistent themes, and one as grimly embedded in the text of *The Spire* as Pangall himself is embedded in the foundations of the cathedral, is the necessity of acquiring knowledge.

The movement from ignorance to revelation is a continual process in Golding's fiction: Ralph's recognition of human evil on the beach in *Lord of the Flies*, Lok's realization that Liku has been eaten in *The Inheritors*, Martin's final knowledge that he is indeed dead in *Pincher Martin*. Jocelin also moves from ignorance to knowledge and, as in Golding's first two novels, it is an act of murder which causes the revelation. However, in certain respects, *The Spire* has as much in common with *Pincher Martin* as it does with the first two novels, not least in that both these books depict the slow, intensely detailed growth of a structure in stone. Simultaneously, because both novels are concerned with portraying a central act of construction, they can be seen as self-reflexive, commenting on their own status as literary texts.

However, there is a significant difference in the symbolic nature of the two structures. In *Pincher Martin*, the rock lacks any symbolic complexity; it is a fantasy conjured up by the memory of a decaying tooth and projected by the protagonist in a desperate attempt to deny death. In its depiction of the spire itself and in its description of the cathedral which supports it, *The Spire* invites symbolic readings in a number of ways:

> The nave was his legs placed together, the transepts on either side were his arms outspread ... And now, also, springing, projecting, bursting, erupting from the heart of the building there was its crown and majesty, the new spire.

It is also possible to see the spire as phallic, as the club with which Jocelin wishes to sexually assault Goody Pangall, but just as the spire itself stands in defiance of logic, so too does *The Spire* refuse to yield to the logic of reductive symbolism.

While *The Spire* and *Pincher Martin* share the same minutely detailed attention to the act of construction, their protagonists also share a characteristic which paradoxically, and probably against the author's intentions, sweeps the reader along with them. Despite the realization that Christopher Martin is a vicious and greedy man, the reader cannot help marvelling at, and admiring, his cornered courage, his relentless will, and his refusal to die. Similarly, while it is made clear from the opening of *The Spire* that Jocelin stands convicted of hubris, the reader marvels at the dean's faith and is overwhelmed by the power and splendour of his vision.

Sacrifice is interwoven throughout *The Spire* with revelation and vision, and when Jocelin realizes his men have sacrificed Pangall, he is stunned by the revelation that he has himself sacrificed Goody. The result of Jocelin's actions, however, cannot change the intensity of the faith which he so obviously possesses, and it is the power of this faith which we are being asked to witness. Golding writes of a faith so strong that its destructive powers amount to what is virtually a blasphemous travesty of faith, yet still remains superior to its antithesis, reason. What appears to be a simple dichotomy between faith and reason, however, is complicated when it is seen that faith in this novel has two guises. The historical setting allows the proximity of Stonehenge to challenge the authority of the cathedral, and just as for *The Inheritors* Golding selected a period of crucial historical importance, the destruction of Neanderthal Man and the simultaneous ascendancy of the New Men, so too in *The Spire* he has chosen a period and a setting which allow him to depict a destructive collision; this time between pagan beliefs and Christianity.

The Spire marks a technical and thematic advance on both *Lord of the Flies* and *The Inheritors*, adding a personal dimension of guilt and knowledge to the revelation of the protagonist, and then subsuming this moment of dual awareness within another, infinitely more complex vision at the novel's conclusion. At the end of the novel, Pangall and Goody are dead, Roger Mason is a hopeless alcoholic, and Jocelin is on his death bed. In the background, the spire still stands. Disturbingly, the reader is asked to consider whether the spire stands despite the sacrifice of Pangall, or because of it. The final moments are another technical triumph for Golding; the highly charged language and the splintered chronology brilliantly evoke the dying moments of Jocelin.

In his last moment of life Jocelin discovers something of immense importance, and simultaneously discovers that what he understands cannot be communicated. Language is an ineffective medium for the communication of what Jocelin has to say, and he is reduced to simile:

> In the tide, flying like a bluebird, struggling, shouting, screaming to leave behind the words of magic and incomprehension –
> *It's like the appletree!*

Jocelin realizes that, like the spire itself, life is a miracle, rooted deeply in both innocence and guilt, in beauty and in blood. *The Spire* both integrates and develops the concerns of its predecessors, and yet it is also prophetic, anticipating several principal concerns of Golding's second phase as a novelist, notably the relationship of language to reality and the ambivalent nature of human experience.

2

Environment and Determinism

Although *The Brass Butterfly* is a comedy, its central concerns are similar to those which appear in the novels. The first performance in Great Britain of the play was at the New Theatre, Oxford, on 24 February 1958. It was directed by Alastair Sim, who also played the Emperor. The play, in three acts, is set in Capri, 'sometime in the 3rd century AD'. Mamillius, the affected and foppish illegitimate grandson of the Emperor, is vainly trying to amuse himself, when two strangers arrive. They are Phanocles, an inventor, and his daughter Euphrosyne, who have come to show the Emperor Phanocles' inventions. The Emperor is particularly impressed with Phanocles' pressure cooker, but the inventor himself is more interested in demonstrating his explosive launcher and his ability to convert a galley into a steam ship. Although the Emperor is deeply suspicious of change, and says, 'Phanocles, in my experience changes have seldom been for the better,' he is persuaded to give Phanocles an old barge which he converts into the warship, *Amphitrite*. The heir designate, Postumus, alarmed at what he takes to be treachery, rushes to Capri to depose Mamillius and the Emperor. During the ensuing violence, *Amphitrite* sinks, set ablaze by the slaves who feared being made redundant by steam. Postumus is killed by an explosion, because the quick-thinking Euphrosyne, with whom Mamillius has somewhat inevitably fallen in love, has removed a safety device, the 'brass butterfly' of the title. In the closing moments of the play, Phanocles demonstrates his own favourite invention: the printing press. Initially impressed by the potential of the invention, the Emperor swiftly revises his opinion and becomes alarmed at the prospect of the proliferation of paper. In order to suppress the invention for as long as possible, he makes Phanocles an ambassador and sends him, with his printing press and gunpowder, on a slow boat to China.

It might seem that Phanocles is being mocked for his rationalist vision of the world, but the Emperor is portrayed as a sensualist whose age now permits him to indulge only in the pleasure of eating, hence his delight in the pressure cooker. It is Phanocles who says to the Emperor: 'My life is passed in a condition of ravished astonishment!' This precludes any suggestion that *The Brass Butterfly* offers a simple dichotomy which is resolved in favour of the Emperor, and this refusal to condemn Phanocles adds a measure of complexity to a work that is too often dismissed as lightweight.

Similarly, the rather arch comedy of the play cannot disguise Golding's characteristically sombre preoccupations. *The Brass Butterfly*, perhaps above all else, is a deeply conservative text; one which echoes *The Inheritors* in its belief that, while change is inevitable, it is more often tragic than purely beneficial. Although the deaths happen off stage, it is an extremely violent play and all the bodies are, ultimately, attributable to the idealistic Phanocles rather than to the cynical and reactionary Emperor. The terrible cost of progress is at the centre of this ostensibly slight comic drama and this issue, along with perennial Golding concerns such as the conflict between the rational and the irrational, and the power of the imaginary over the actual, is also found throughout the collection of three novellas Golding published in 1971 entitled *The Scorpion God*.

It would be surprising if at least one of these three stories did not have something in common with *The Brass Butterfly*. Golding first published the story 'Envoy Extraordinary' in a collection entitled *Sometime, Never: Three Tales of Imagination* (1956), which also included stories by John Wyndham and Mervyn Peake. He later turned 'Envoy Extraordinary' into a radio play for the BBC, and then, changing the title, expanded it into *The Brass Butterfly*. The other two stories, 'Clonk Clonk' and 'The Scorpion God', although set in very different times and places, also take the issue of progress as their principal subject. 'The Scorpion God' seems to be set in Egypt, probably in the late Middle Kingdom and it opens with a detached, almost cinematic view of an Egyptian king. He is called 'Great House', a translation of the title 'Pharaoh', and he is running. It soon becomes clear that this race is a ritual; one that takes place every seven years and which is designed to ensure that the river will rise, thereby guaranteeing prosperity for all. If the king does not finish the race, or the river does not rise high enough, the king will be put to death. However, this practice does not simply mean the death of one person, for when the king dies his entire household is put to death with him. This ancient custom is quite satisfactory to everybody, except to the character known as the Liar.

The Liar is an outsider, possibly a Syrian, and he is an Egyptian version of a court jester. He amuses Great House with his stories of a world outside the rigidly circumscribed one the Egyptians know: a world of snow, of white-skinned people, and, most unbelievable of all, a world where people have sexual relationships only with those to whom they are unrelated. Incest is at the centre of Egyptian life and Great House is supposed to sleep with his own daughter, Princess Pretty Flower, but is too drunk and lazy to perform the act. The Head Man recognizes that this failure is symbolic, and the king is put to death. The Liar, however, refuses to accept the honour of accompanying his master to the tomb and so he is thrown into the pit.

Although everything has been done according to custom, the river continues to rise and, when the Head Man investigates the possible causes for this, he discovers that the Liar has been having an affair with the Princess. He orders the Liar to be taken from the pit and insists that he join Great House in death. But the Liar escapes, killing the Head Man in the process. The story ends with the Princess suggesting to those around her that they had better go and talk to him. 'The Scorpion God' is considerably more complex than it may at first appear. Incest is at the centre of the story and functions not only as a plot device but also as a metaphor for the enclosed and unhealthily insular world of the Egyptians. The story seems to offer the reader an oppositional conflict between the sterile, death-obsessed vision of life held by the Egyptians and the life-affirming, healthy vision of the world held by the Liar. Golding's work often features a conflict between the rational and the irrational, but in 'The Scorpion God' the lines between the two are blurred in a way they are not, for example, in *The Spire*. In that novel, Roger Mason symbolizes Reason while Jocelin represents Faith. Here, however, the conflict is personified in the characters of the Head Man and the Liar, and both are, in their different ways, rational men. The Head Man believes the river's rise cannot be causally linked to snow melting in the south because that would mean that the south had a warmer sun than their own hot land, in which no snow ever falls. This may be, it turns out, incorrect, but it is not illogical.

The Liar is necessary; it is he, or someone like him, who will devise methods of taming nature rather than meekly succumbing to its dictates, but, as always in Golding's fiction, there is a price to pay. The Liar has lost his belief in the harmonious structure of the universe. When told by the Head Man to think of 'real things', the Liar says 'Death. Murder. Lust. The pit.' Against this, the Egyptians celebrate an unfathomable mystery at the centre of human existence. The conflict in 'The Scorpion God' is similar to that portrayed in *The Brass Butterfly*; humanity must progress, change is inevitable, but there is always a heavy price to pay. The Liar, paradoxically, tells 'the Truth', but in Golding's fiction there is more to life than empirically apprehended truth, and his own imaginative sympathies lie with the Egyptians.

'Clonk Clonk' is a comic tale, and probably the most optimistic piece of fiction that Golding has ever published. It is set one hundred thousand years ago, almost certainly in Africa. There are clear similarities with *The Inheritors*, but significant differences also, not least in the comedy and optimism of the story. The story is predicated almost entirely upon the emphatic distinctions between men and women, and their separate spheres of influence, but concludes with an act of reconciliation between the two genders. 'Clonk Clonk' has two principal characters: Palm, the Head Woman, and Chimp, a flute-playing male, whose weak ankle keeps him from fully participating in the masculine activity of hunting.

Again, the story is far from complex. 'Clonk Clonk' is divided into six sections, and the first four of these alternate between the lives of the women and those of the men. Although the story has an omniscient narrator, the thoughts and observations of Palm dominate the women's section and through these we learn that it is the women who perform virtually all the important functions of the tribe. The men do little else but hunt and the women, at least among themselves, regard them as children, although they shamelessly flatter male vanity and express considerable deference in public to keep the peace. From the beginning of the story, Palm is seen to be directly involved with birth and mating and death. Palm is also known within the tribe as 'She Who Names The Women', and an important distinction between male and female attitudes towards names emerges in the opening pages of the story.

The women are named after fish, trees, and flowers, and once Palm has given a woman her name it never changes. Throughout the story, women are associated with custom and memory. Conversely, the men's names, which are those of the animals they hunt, change constantly, in response to whatever significant event has just occurred. Chimp begins the story as Charging Elephant, suffers the indignity of being renamed Charging Elephant Fell On His Face In Front Of An Antelope, is then called Chimp and driven away, and finally, as Palm's man, is named Water Paw! Wounded Leopard! Excitable, child-like, aggressive, volatile, the men are also capable of adapting quickly to change, and they welcome Chimp back into the group with the same ease they had rejected him.

The first four sections are devoted to establishing an absolute polarity between men and women. While the women brew alcohol, plant crops and organize the camp, the men are out hunting. During the hunt Chimp is driven off for his weaknesses as a hunter, but it is he who leads the tribe to the leopard which they kill. They acknowledge this and even wonder where he is, forgetting already that they have just driven him away. The fifth and sixth sections describe the breakdown of the polarities between men and women. Chimp, alone, creeps back to the camp where the women are drunkenly enjoying themselves under a full moon. Chimp finds Palm and they sleep together. In the morning Chimp explains his weakness to her: 'Clonk. My ankle says clonk'; to which she replies: 'And I go clonk inside'. Male and Female here have come to complement one another, externally and internally, rather than existing in antithetical positions. When Palm publicly announces that Chimp is her man, the reconciliation of ostensible opposites is complete.

Chimp is also a musician, and it is, ultimately, his unique gifts as an artist which bring about the harmonious resolution. The story can then be seen as a fable about the role of the artist in society. Like the other stories in this collection, 'Clonk Clonk' has some wonderful comic moments, but unlike 'The Scorpion God' and 'Envoy Extraordinary', this story seems strongly optimistic in its suggestion that some changes are certainly for the better.

Change, and stasis, are at the centre of *The Pyramid* (1967), the only novel Golding published during this phase of his career. Although the book shows the reader a town which celebrates stasis, the text itself has undergone considerable changes of its own – and some critics argue that *The Pyramid* cannot be seen as a novel at all. Two of the three sections which comprise the book appeared separately in different publications: the first was published as 'On the Escarpment' in the *Kenyon Review* (June 1967), and the third section was published as 'Inside a Pyramid' in *Esquire* (December 1966). The three episodes are distinct, yet considerable continuity is provided by the same characters' appearance throughout all three sections, and, in particular, by Oliver, the book's first person narrator.

The first section places the young Oliver in the small, stiflingly claustrophobic English town of Stilbourne. Many English place names do indeed end in 'bourne', but rarely with such neat metaphorical applicability as occurs in *The Pyramid*. Stilbourne is almost certainly Marlborough, where Golding lived during his own childhood and adolescence, just as Barchester in *The Spire* is recognizably Salisbury, where Golding also lived for many years. The novel's title and the epigraph continue Golding's life-long preoccupation with Egypt. The epigraph, taken from *The Instructions of Ptah-Hotep*, reads: 'If thou be among people make for thyself love, the beginning and end of the heart.' The title has obvious connections with Egypt, but these connections may well work in more than one way. A pyramid is a traditional image for representing a class structure, and *The Pyramid* is very clearly a novel about social class. Oliver's father is Stilbourne's chemist, and the family occupy an uneasy and never quite defined position within the social hierarchy.

Oliver's desire for Evie Babbacombe, the daughter of the caretaker of the town hall, is complicated by the similar desires of Bobby Ewan, whose father is the doctor. While Oliver goes to the local grammar school, Bobby goes to a boarding school. Oliver is chunkily built, Bobby is thin with 'the Duke of Wellington's profile'. As an adolescent, Oliver thinks back to an exchange between himself and Bobby as children:

> 'You're my slave.'
> 'No I'm not.'
> 'Yes you are. My father's a doctor and yours is only his dispenser.'

Although Evie, Oliver and Bobby are all from different positions within the social pyramid, they do not neatly represent the lower, middle and upper classes. Within *The Pyramid*, the social differences between the two boys symbolize perhaps the most bitterly disputed demarcation line within the English class system; the one between the upper and the lower middle classes.

Pyramids, however, are not only apt metaphors for evaluating hierarchical structures, they are also suggestive of death; an embalmed, somewhat eerie sort of death. *The Pyramid* depicts a world of crushing mediocrity, and Stilbourne is a society which is paralysed to the point of immobility by its obsession with class and the niceties of social behaviour. Stilbourne is a town in love with death rather than life, and it resists change with all the murderously genteel weapons that it possesses. Oliver's sexual escapades with Evie allow him to transcend the class barriers, but in doing this he uses Evie in a way that diminishes her unique human identity. Their relationship appears a straightforward one. Oliver is consumed with lust for her, much as Mountjoy was for Beatrice in *Free Fall*, and *The Pyramid* is brilliantly comic in its depiction of the young and lustful Oliver. But when Oliver contemplates having to marry Evie, he thinks only of the social *status quo* and the irreparable and unforgivable damage he would inflict upon it by so rash an act.

Golding adds a coda to the first section, much as he had done in his earlier novels, moving forward two years to show Oliver and Evie in a Stilbourne pub. In the course of the evening, Evie gets her revenge on Oliver by publicly announcing that he had once tried to rape her. In parting, she also implies that her relationship with her father was incestuous; an issue which links *The Pyramid* with 'The Scorpion God'. Although Oliver has returned from Oxford, it is significant that none of the book's three sections show him there; all his real learning experiences occur in Stilbourne.

In the second section of the novel, the production of *King of Hearts* is used to further Oliver's understanding of the complexity of life and the impoverishment of lives, including his own, which are locked into debilitating notions of what constitutes 'acceptable' behaviour. The initial letters of the Stilbourne Operatic Society spell out an ironic message; ironic because there are no souls to save in Stilbourne. Music is one of the central issues within *The Pyramid* and, in an interview with James Baker, Golding explained that the book has a musical structure. It is based on a sonata form, with the middle section as a scherzo, or a comic commentary on the rest of the piece. The book's principal preoccupations are all present in the second chapter – class, sex, music – but there is an element of broad farce running through it which mocks Oliver's own seriousness about such issues.

Imogen Grantley replaces Evie Babbacombe as Oliver's focus of desire, but the show's director, Evelyn De Tracey, shows Oliver Imogen's fundamental mediocrity, and also the limitations and the spiritual and intellectual deadness of Stilbourne itself. When a drunken Oliver tells De Tracey he wants to learn 'the *truth* of things', the even drunker director passes him a photo of himself wearing a woman's clothes. The callow and sheltered Oliver can respond only with uproarious laughter. His recognition of human vulnerability comes too late for him to apologize and, although the chapter ends with Oliver stepping in front of the audience to take his bows, he is bitterly aware that he is undeserving of any applause.

The third section describes Oliver, now middle aged and prosperous, returning to Stilbourne. The chapter is heavily retrospective, dwelling principally on the young Oliver's relationship with his music teacher, Bounce Dawlish. Oliver has long renounced his own passion for music in favour of a successful career as an industrial chemist, and the chapter is overwhelmingly concerned with the issues of renunciation, loss, and regret. However, it opens with images of progress and of success. Henry Williams, who begins the novel as an itinerant handyman, now seems to own most of Stilbourne. His success, of course, is built on Bounce's destruction. Just as Oliver turned Evie into an object for his own pleasure, so Henry ruthlessly exploits the lonely Bounce.

As Oliver looks at Henry's inscription on Bounce's tombstone, 'Heaven is music', the grim irony of it forces him to acknowledge that, contrary to everybody's beliefs, he had always disliked her. The narrative perspective in this chapter is the most sophisticated in the novel, combining Oliver's youthful memories with an adult's understanding. This double voice is used to particularly good effect as Oliver remembers the occasion when Bounce walked, virtually naked, into the town square, in a doomed and pathetic bid to gain Henry's attention. As with the Evie and De Tracey scenes, Oliver learns of the pain and sorrow that underlie people's lives. He also learns a truth about himself. The character in Stilbourne he most resembles is Henry, a point deftly made in the closing lines of the novel. The last transaction between the two men is a commercial one. As Henry goes to change Oliver's money, Oliver feels that if only he could make a *difference*, he would pay 'anything – *anything*', but in the same instant he knows that 'like Henry, I would never pay more than a reasonable price'. When Henry returns with his change Oliver looks him in the eye – and sees his own face. Oliver drives away in his 'car of superior description' and doesn't look back.

Oliver is a success, but he has paid the price. He has renounced his musical gifts for a prosperous career as a manufacturer of poison gas. *The Pyramid*'s somewhat lifeless prose style perfectly complements Stilbourne life, and makes it clear that Oliver is one of the town's most representative citizens. He has not, appearances to the contrary, escaped from Stilbourne; the town has made him a man who will never pay more than a reasonable price. The novel's preoccupation with survival and the price it exacts links it to *The Inheritors*, *The Spire*, *The Brass Butterfly*, 'The Scorpion God', and, to some degree, to virtually all of Golding's fiction. However, this does not diminish the originality of *The Pyramid*. By setting the novel in so genteel an environment Golding is able to emphasize the brutally destructive effects of the English class system. He also suggests, as he will do later in *Rites of Passage*, that negotiating its complexities can often literally be a matter of life or death.

Although Golding is primarily known as a writer of fiction, he has also published two volumes of essays and a travel journal: *The Hot Gates* (1965), *A Moving Target* (1982), and *An Egyptian Journal* (1985). There are a number of years separating the publication of each of these three books, but as they are Golding's only non-fiction it seems appropriate to evaluate them together. The voice which emerges from these books of essays is often comic, with a droll wit, and the range of Golding's preoccupations is itself fascinating. Overall, the essays have received very little critical attention, and when they are discussed at all only those which seem to have a direct bearing on his fiction have engaged critics. However, everything Golding has written is of interest and virtually any one of his essays can illuminate his fiction.

In 'My First Book', from *A Moving Target*, Golding writes of his early love of poetry, and in particular of the resonant phrase. He notes: 'It would be a phrase that recreated by some magic the phenomenon that lay under its hand.' Golding sees 'the thing in itself', a phrase he takes from the philosopher Immanuel Kant, as always obscured, and it is natural then that he would be attracted to fable, where one narrative level clearly obscures another one, the 'real' one. The process by which the real is uncovered is, for

Golding, always a magical, or imaginative, process.

In 'My First Book', Golding says of himself: 'I have always been a curious mixture of conservative and anarchist', and both collections show this to be true. As with his fiction, the subject matter of his essays often reveals a conservative turn of mind, but his interest in form shows his radicalism. An essay such as 'Body and Soul', in *The Hot Gates*, for example, is written with considerable flair and imagination. The mildly hysterical and jerky prose style is designed to evoke the frenzied pace of modern air travel, and increasingly, through the cumulative effect of hundreds of grammatically unfulfilled sentences and phrases, as well as a confusing alternation between present and past tenses, the reader begins to share the author's sense of unreality. Similarly, the artful use of rhetorical questions in 'The English Channel', again from *The Hot Gates*, forces the reader to share the author's questions, rather than accepting his conclusions.

In a sense there are no 'minor' essays in either of the two collections, as invariably the lesser-known essays offer fascinatingly oblique comments on the novels. In *The Hot Gates*, 'A Touch of Insomnia' describes a sea voyage, but this time the piece evolves into a meditation on the English class system and on the nature of time. 'Crosses', from the same collection is a comic article about Golding's chief dislikes and irritations, but it ends by speculating on the phenomenon of human cruelty. 'Through the Dutch Waterways', from *A Moving Target*, begins as a straightforward travel piece but becomes a sustained speculation on the national differences between the Dutch and the English. Similarly, his reviews of specific books and writers become general meditations on good and evil, the power of art, and the redemptive possibilities of the imagination. His views are often challenging and unconventional. In *A Moving Target* he reviews Iona and Peter Opie's *The Classic Fairy Tales* and in the course of his review he rejects the belief that fairy stories are primarily of value in instilling children with moral values. He writes that, instead, such stories liberate children 'from obsession with the commonplace', and goes on to say of them: 'They pose us a paradox, a contradiction, and in the end they do not explain it so much as resolve it like discord.' This comment could be made of Golding's own fiction, which often shares something of the mythic nature of fairy stories. His interest in scientists and astronomers, his fondness for archaeology and engineering, similarly indicate a fascination with scale, with power, with the visionary, which is actually motivated by the poetic impulse, not the scientific. A pattern begins to emerge: what Golding does extremely well in the shorter pieces and reviews from both books is move from the particular to the general, something he has been doing in his fiction since *Lord of the Flies*.

The Hot Gates is made up of a number of articles, travel pieces and book reviews first published in the *Spectator*, *Holiday Magazine*, the *Times Literary Supplement* and the *Listener*. The book also contains a lecture, 'Fable' and three autobiographical essays: 'Egypt from My Inside', 'The Ladder and the Tree' and 'Billy the Kid'. Because they seem most relevant to the fiction, it is these autobiographical essays that are most commonly discussed. It is true that 'Billy the Kid', for example, is an interesting evocation of Golding's childhood, but it is difficult to see how this essay tells us any more about Golding's view of life than does, say, the title essay of the book. 'The Hot Gates' is an account of Golding's journey to Greece to retrace the route of the Persian invasion in 480 BC, and in particular to look at the pass where Leonidas and his Spartans held the Persians. It is entertainingly written and historically informative, but its real interest for the admirer of Golding's fiction may well reside in the author's understanding of the soldiers who were guarding the pass and of the way in which all wars are fought. Golding writes, 'That is the one certain thing – the mixed force was quarrelling', while a little later he refers to 'the inevitable traitor'.

Golding is 'certain' the force was quarrelling and he describes a traitor as 'inevitable'. The essay gradually reveals a pessimistic, deterministic, and highly conservative view of human nature which is similar to that expressed in his fiction. Golding has little sympathy with the contemporary view, heavily influenced by the emergence of sociology as a discipline, which sees most human nature as culturally determined, created by social circumstances. Golding's essentialism is revealed more clearly in an essay such as this than in any of his novels because there is no detached narrative perspective, just the voice of the writer responding to one of the most important events in Western history. Golding acknowledges that Leonidas and the Spartans 'contributed to set us free', and he concludes by paraphrasing for us the stark simplicity of the Spartans' epitaph, finishing the essay humbly, subduing his own voice.

This is not, of course, to say that the autobiographical essays in *The Hot Gates* are without interest. Of the three, 'Egypt from My Inside' is perhaps the most fascinating, but Golding reprinted it in *A Moving Target* and it is more useful to look at it next to 'Egypt from My Outside', published for the first time in that collection. As noted earlier, 'Billy the Kid' is an evocative account of Golding's childhood, but it also celebrates the ostensibly paradoxical temperament of the young Golding, passionately in love with words, and passionately fond of fighting. These two obsessions, language and violence, are at the centre of everything he has written. 'The Ladder and the Tree' is a more sophisticated essay, and relies more heavily on the creation of dual levels of meaning: the actual and the metaphorical. The specific, autobiographical details of the piece seem less important than the discovery of horror and mystery which the young Golding sees as lying all about him, and which he realizes are to play an important role in his life.

The 'tree' in this essay is the literal one in which the young Golding sits and reads, and, on one level, reading and imagination are the principal themes of the essay. The 'ladder' is a literal one, which Golding's helpful, rational father builds for him, so he can climb the tree, and which his son deliberately breaks so as to make the ascent into his tree more romantically arduous. But it is also, metaphorically, education, in its most dreary and unimaginative aspect: 'Rules, declensions, paradigms and vocabularies stretched before me. They were like a ladder which I knew now I should climb, rung after factual rung ...' This shift from the actual to the metaphorical is a consistent feature of Golding's essays; the glass door, in the essay of the same name, is both an actual door which Golding opens to go into the library, and a metaphor for emphasizing the separate lives that exist on either side of the door and which constantly remain in full view of one another. 'The Ladder and the Tree' is structured around the conflict between the pragmatic and the imaginative, between the rational and the irrational – themes which have preoccupied Golding throughout his adult life.

While 'The Hot Gates' is often not read at all, 'An Affection for Cathedrals', from *A Moving Target*, is usually read in too blinkered a fashion – as a way of learning something useful about *The Spire*. But this essay is also an excellent example of Golding's ability imaginatively to re-create an older age, and of his unconventional and stimulating perspective. He goes on from a discussion of 'laughable' Winchester statues to look at a tribute to William Walker, a diver who 'worked daily for six years, in slime and stinking darkness, until he had underpinned the walls and made the cathedral safe'. Ultimately, the essay criticizes, as does so much of Golding's work, the 'sane, sadness' of rationalism, and celebrates power and mystery.

This theme re-emerges throughout *A Moving Target* whenever Golding discusses literature. 'Intimate Relations', for example, is an assessment of journal keeping and the people who keep them, and Golding ends his survey without arriving at any conclusions, subtextually implying that the journal form asks more questions than it can ever answer. This belief in the mystery of human existence and the inexplicability of certain events is an issue he returns to in *Rites of Passage*. Similarly, in 'Rough Magic', Golding discusses the work of a number of novelists (James, Steinbeck, Austen, Joyce, Thackeray), and his approach throughout is professional and analytical. However, he concludes by announcing that critical analysis cannot account for everything, an issue which he re-investigates in *The Paper Men*: 'For all the complexity of literature there is a single focus in literature, a point of the blazing human will. This is where definition and explanation break down. We must call on a higher language.' The desire to avoid the reductive plays a large part in Golding's work, and is the reason for his irascible comment in 'Belief and Creativity' that 'Marx, Darwin and Freud are the three most crashing bores of the Western world'. These three thinkers, Golding believes, are themselves reductive, turning the mystery of life into that which can be apprehended by logic and reason alone. It is his refusal to accept so limited a view that lies behind his announcement in 'Egypt from My Inside' that he is himself 'an Ancient Egyptian, with all their unreason, spiritual pragmatism, and capacity for ambiguous and even contradictory belief.' This essay and its companion piece, 'Egypt from My Outside', are probably Golding's most popular essays and the principal dynamic of both is the celebration of mystery.

The Hot Gates contains twenty separate entries and *A Moving Target* has seventeen, but all of the pieces can be seen to share a very few central preoccupations. One of the most persistent concerns of both volumes of essays is the way in which the imaginary is invariably, and against all expectations, superior to the actual. All of the travel pieces, especially 'The Hot Gates', 'Shakespeare's Birthplace', 'Egypt from My Outside' and 'Delphi', are centred around this notion, while it is a persistent theme within *An Egyptian Journal*. 'Egypt from My Inside' is an account of Golding's life-long fascination with the *idea* of Egypt; 'Egypt from My Outside' is an account of the *reality* of the country. The former essay recounts the young Golding's visit to the British Museum, where he is befriended by a curator who allows him actually to touch one of the mummies. The description of this moment is extraordinarily evocative: 'and at last I laid my compelled, my quivering and sacrilegious hand on the thing in itself, experienced beyond all Kantian question, the bone, and its binding of thick, leathery skin'. Moments later, Golding admits that none of this happened at all. The form of the essay, in which an imaginary experience is offered within what is represented as a real account, perfectly complements Golding's theme. It is striking that the most powerful experience within the essay never really happened; once again the reader is being shown the superiority of the imaginary over the actual. 'Egypt from My Inside' rejects dull methodology and the unimaginative use of statistics to comprehend the Egyptians, and instead endorses the limitless potential of the human spirit, the force of mystery and myth, which they and their legacy represent.

'Egypt from My Outside' is an account of Golding's actual trip to Egypt, accompanied by his wife, in the winter of 1976. It is impressively and evocatively written, full of good humour and shrewd insights, and was initially delivered as a lecture, but like its predecessor it is also composed of two different narratives. The first is his retrospective description of the journey, and the second narrative consists of extracts from the journal Golding kept during the trip. The continuous alternation between the two allows Golding to emphasize the central concern of his essay: the way in which, without imagination on the part of the traveller, the actuality of even the most ancient monument is attenuated, can even be a disappointment. Once again, the power of the imagination is privileged over the apprehension of the real. As might be expected, the same theme emerges from the travel book, *An Egyptian Journal*.

This full-length work describes Golding's trip to Egypt nearly ten years later, but this time in a boat, cruising on the Nile, again accompanied by his wife. Golding was a serious sailor himself and the book is particularly good on nautical details, especially the complex business of navigation. There are some wonderful moments in *An Egyptian Journal*. Golding's descriptive powers add poetry to a number of situations and there are some beautiful photographs, many of them taken by Golding himself. However, it is difficult not to agree with those contemporary reviewers who felt that Golding's gifts were not particularly well suited to the full-length travel book. His shorter pieces are enjoyable because of their brevity; they achieve their effect through an economy of language and narrow focus which selects a crucial incident and extrapolates from it. There is often too much detail in *An Egyptian Journal*, and too little analysis of what has been seen. It is significant that the two most memorable moments in the book can be said not to have really happened at all, just as occurs in 'Egypt from My Inside'.

In the first of these incidents Golding hears of a tourist who has fallen to his death at the temple of Kom Ombo. Immediately, he begins to construct a history for the unfortunate traveller: assuming him to be a man, imagining a wife who has stayed behind at the hotel, possibly with a headache. It is the instinctive act of a novelist, as Golding himself wryly acknowledges, yet it is, in its way, 'truer' than many of the descriptions of towns and landscapes which have preceded it. The other telling incident is near the end of the book when Golding anticipates going to Oxyrhynchus. He allows his imagination full rein as he contemplates this mysterious site and in his mind he rewrites the history of early Christianity. His language moves toward the rhapsodic, and he concludes his reverie with these remarkable words: 'I remember coming to Memphis thousands of years ago in the area opposite where Cairo would be but was yet undreamed of ...' It is an extraordinarily powerful scene, and yet, as Golding writes in the earlier essay, 'none of the episode happened at all'. The role of the imagination, and particularly the imaginative power of art, plays a large part in the third phase of Golding's writing.

3

Distinctions and Denials

Although the chronology of the novels Golding published in the last fourteen years of his life is *Darkness Visible* (1979), *Rites of Passage* (1980), *The Paper Men* (1984), *Close Quarters* (1987), *Fire Down Below* (1989), it seems appropriate to assess the novels outside this order. The second, fourth and fifth of these novels form a trilogy, known either as 'The Sea Trilogy', or by the title given to the trilogy when it was published in a single volume in 1991: *To the Ends of the Earth*. The narrative continuity of the trilogy means it would be more useful to assess all three novels together, so this last section will consider *Darkness Visible* and *The Paper Men* before the trilogy, which allows me to conclude with an assessment of the last novel Golding published in his lifetime.

By the late 1970s it was generally felt that Golding was a spent force, that he had taken his unique vision as far as it could go. Then, in 1979, *Darkness Visible* was published, an event which demonstrated that Golding still had one of the most extraordinary voices in contemporary literature. In general, the book was received enthusiastically, but with some bewilderment. The author himself did nothing to clear up the confusion by his refusal to speak about the novel at all. Golding had been an unusually co-operative author in terms of discussing his own work, as he was about subsequent books, and this quite uncharacteristic reticence on his part has contributed a great deal to the mystique which still surrounds the novel.

Darkness Visible has a straightforward enough story line. It is divided into three sections, each one of which is centred upon a specific character. The first section focuses upon Matty, who has emerged from the blazing ruins of London's docks after a bombing raid during World War II, and who acts throughout the novel like an Old Testament prophet. Matty tends to be seen as a figure representing 'Good'. The second section centres upon Sophy who, because of her criminal behaviour, sexual excesses, and general attitude to life, tends to be seen as the antithesis of Matty, and therefore as a figure representing 'Evil'. The third section describes the coming together of these two characters. Sophy plans to kidnap a child for ransom from the school where Matty is working as a caretaker, but Matty sacrifices his life to prevent this from happening. The novel ends with the death of Mr Pedigree, a paedophile, who once taught Matty and who appears throughout the novel as both a tragic and a comic figure.

Darkness Visible is seen by most critics as Golding's 'condition of England' novel, and there is a similar consensus regarding the book's title, which, although unacknowledged in Golding's text, is assumed to be taken from Milton's *Paradise Lost*: 'No light, but rather darkness visible | Served only to discover sights of woe' (Bk I, ll. 63–4). Milton here is describing Hell, as Satan surveys his new kingdom after being expelled with all his minions from Heaven. The assumption that Golding is indebted to Milton for his title leads to the inevitable assumption that the novel portrays modern England as a kind of Hell.

However, although Golding would never talk about *Darkness Visible*, he did make a general comment about his own fiction which could be seen as a rebuttal of the pervasive belief that the novel is an attempt to present England's contemporary moral disintegration. He said in an interview with James Wood in the *Guardian*: 'I wouldn't know how to begin to write about contemporary society.' In addition, it is worth noting that the phrase 'darkness visible' also appears in Pope's poem *The Dunciad*: 'Of darkness visible so much be lent | As half to show, half veil, the deep intent' (Bk IV, ll. 3–4). When *Paradise Lost* is no longer seen as the only possible source for the title of *Darkness Visible* it becomes possible to see the book in different ways. It could actually be argued that *Darkness Visible* is not particularly concerned with moral issues at all, but is primarily concerned with the act of 'seeing'. The emphasis within the title can fall on 'visible', not 'darkness', and this then complements Pope's phrase 'half to show, half veil'. When looked at in this way, the novel seems to imply that 'good' and 'evil' are evaluations primarily based on perception, rather than absolute moral values.

While *The Spire* represents Faith and Reason engaged in a persistent struggle, and emphasizes their opposing natures, *Darkness Visible* shows Good and Evil as completely interdependent, the one incapable of existing without the other. Matty and

Sophy can be seen as representing a relationship similar to that which is expressed in the concept of *yin* and *yang*. In *Irrational Man* (New York, 1958) William Barrett described it thus:

> ... the famous diagram of the forces of *yin* and *yang*, in which the light and the dark lie down beside each other within the same circle, the dark area penetrated by a spot of light and the light by a spot of dark, to symbolize that each must borrow from the other, that the light has need of the dark, and conversely, in order for either to be complete. (p.73)

The central movement within *Darkness Visible* is toward reconciliation, and the idea of unity is pervasive throughout the novel. It is worth noting that the novel's unacknowledged epigraph is taken from Virgil's *Aeneid* and with Dryden's translation of this book an extremely powerful vision of unity is presented:

> Know first, that Heav'n, and Earth's compacted Frame,
> And flowing Waters, and the starry Flame,
> And both the Radiant Lights, one Common Soul
> Inspires, and feeds, and animates the whole.
>
> (Bk VI, ll. 980–3)

One of the most striking features of *Darkness Visible* is the manner in which dual levels of meaning are always clearly apparent. When Matty begins work at Frankley's, for example, a description of the way money is conveyed through the shop can immediately be seen as an ingenious metaphor to describe a society so complex that, while it interacts and connects on every level, it paradoxically tends to isolate its inhabitants: 'This complex machinery had been designed as a method of preventing each shop assistant from having his own till. The unforeseen result was that the spider's web isolated the assistants.'

Similarly, immediately before Matty is attacked by Harry Bummer in Australia, Golding writes: 'The fall made him breathless and for a moment among the wheeling rays and flashes from the meridian there seemed to be a darkness, man-shaped and huge.' The word 'fall' here can be seen to function in precisely the same way that it is used throughout *The Inheritors* – both on the level of narrative realism and also on a specifically metaphorical level, as when Lok says of the new people: 'they are a people of the fall; nothing stands against them'. Harry Bummer is presented as a dramatization of Cardinal Newman's famous assertion that mankind has been implicated in some 'terrible aboriginal calamity'. That the darkness here is 'man-shaped' implies that evil resides in humanity's innermost nature, and that Harry represents the flesh which keeps humanity from fulfilling its spiritual desires, an argument supported by Matty's earlier thoughts on castration, before he encounters Harry.

While there is always another level of meaning present within the novel, it is structurally uncomplicated. This structural simplicity, however, is often obscured by the complicated narrative perspective, as invariably occurs in Golding's fiction. In this case, the interaction of different narrative voices and perspectives works toward establishing the difficulty, even the impossibility, of seeing what is 'really' present. The first section of the novel, for example, is comprised of Matty's consciousness, the perspective of the subsidiary characters, and the voice of the narrator. Initially, these appear as three clearly distinct narrative perspectives, and the moments during which the reader receives impressions which are being presented through Matty's singular perceptions, for example, are obvious: '... and beyond it was a tall tree full of angels'. Similarly, it is not very difficult, most of the time, to distinguish between the different voices of the various characters and of the narrator. But it is not always possible to separate the various narrative voices so confidently. The following comment, for example, appears to belong to the third voice, that of the omniscient narrator: 'When she did that it was the first time since his emergence from the furnace that he was observed to employ the complex musculature of his face in a communicative way.' A closer consideration of the terminology, however, suggests that the perspective is that of the medical staff who are treating Matty. The statement is comprised of two different perspectives, and this blurring of ostensibly emphatic distinctions is a striking attribute of Matty himself, who shifts, for example, between different biblical personas. This haziness can also be seen in terms of the novel's tone.

Darkness Visible is often humorous and the great majority of comic moments are created by the sardonic voice of the narrator intruding decisively into the text: 'He busied himself with the kind of first aid for burns which is reversed by the medical profession every year or so.' But appalling things happen in *Darkness Visible*, and the comedy of the novel is consistently juxtaposed with the tragic and the grotesque, so that eventually the distinctions between tragedy and comedy begin to blur, evidence again of the novel's denial of distinctions. The comedy in the novel is thematic because *Darkness Visible* is concerned not only with the horror and banality of life, but also with the splendour and comedy of life; with life as a totality, as One.

The contemporary setting of *Darkness Visible* is often stressed by the novel's readers, but one of the implications which arises from this recognition has an almost syllogistic inevitability to it. The modern world is evil, Sophy is a true child of the modern world, therefore Sophy is evil. While such a thought process may not always be consciously articulated, it may still be of some significance in establishing and maintaining the prevailing critical view of Sophy. Sophy's actions, because morally wrong, result in a distinction being drawn by the reader between Matty and Sophy, when throughout the novel Sophy (whose name means 'divine wisdom') is actually engaged in the same spiritual quest as Matty.

Sophy is certainly attracted to the darker side of life, but Golding, like W. B. Yeats in his 'Crazy Jane' poems, suggests that vision and revelation are not confined to the world of church pews and conventional piety. Matty and Sophy are far more alike than they are opposed and many of Sophy's ostensibly cruel and pointless actions have a supernatural or mystical element within them. For example, in the 'dabchick incident', when Sophy kills the bird, she is shown experimenting with a form of magic, just as Matty does on a number of occasions.

While the very mystery of his origins effectively precludes any psychological dimension to Matty's character, Sophy possesses a psychological depth far in excess of any other character within *Darkness Visible*, and this complexity is principally generated by the ambivalent relationship she has with her father. Sophy's feelings for her father cannot be divided specifically into either 'hate' or 'love'; neither word adequately indicates the immense force and the irrational, somehow fated nature of Sophy's relationship with her father. There are strong overtones of incestuous desire in the episodes focusing upon Mr Stanhope and Sophy, and it is possible that incest here functions as a form of metaphor, as a way of incorporating into the novel's interrogation of binary oppositions the specific sexual distinction that should exist between parent and child in our culture.

The novel consistently suggests that barriers and partitions are made by humanity and therefore can be broken down, but only Matty seems to attain this desirable unity in any permanent sense, and he pays a price which is absolute. Although *Darkness Visible* promotes an Ideal, therefore, it actually depicts a fragmentary and imperfect reality. Sim receives an apprehension of harmonious unity during which all partitions disappear, but it is confined to a single moment. Matty ascends gloriously into a state of spiritual unity, and yet Matty is the only character within the novel to take another life. Sophy escapes unpunished and so does Toni. Sim receives spiritual awareness ahead of his more morally upright friend, Edwin. Sim's son remains in an asylum and Henderson remains a corpse. It is perhaps not surprising that Golding refused to talk about so morally ambivalent and deeply disturbing a book as *Darkness Visible*, but it is ironic, as the control an author has over his work is a central concern of *The Paper Men*.

The Paper Men was very poorly received when it appeared in 1984, attracting the worst reviews of Golding's career. The novel describes the efforts of an elderly novelist, Wilf Barclay, to escape the predatory attempts of a young American academic, Rick Tucker, who wishes to write a biography of Barclay. Perhaps understandably, *The Paper Men* was seen as a rather cantankerous attack on academics by a famous author, and, perhaps equally understandably, academics and reviewers were not particularly amused. However, like *Darkness Visible, The Paper Men* clearly operates on more than the one level. Again like *Darkness Visible*, the novel presents the reader with a binary opposition which over the course of the novel is seen to be illusory. In *Darkness Visible* the antithesis that is destroyed is the one believed to exist between Good and Evil, while in *The Paper Men* the binary opposition which is similarly denied is the one held to exist between 'creative' and 'critical' writing. This notion is then further developed to affirm the same central premise as underlies *Darkness Visible*: the belief that Good and Evil are the same phenomenon. While *Darkness Visible* assesses the role of the 'seer' in modern society, *The Paper Men* assesses the role of the artist.

The Paper Men does, initially at least, appear to contain a vicious attack on literary criticism and critics, and certainly the majority of readers unquestioningly assume that Barclay speaks for Golding. Confusingly, there are grounds for initially assuming this to be so. In the title piece of his second volume of essays, Golding writes: 'I was a structuralist at the age of seven, which is about the right age for it', while in *The Paper Men* Barclay says of a woman at the conference, '... but she proved to a serious academic and a structuralist to boot'. Paradoxically, and ingeniously, however, in this novel Golding actually agrees with several of the most contentious theories advanced by post-war literary criticism, particularly the notion that there is no significant difference between 'creative' writing and 'critical' writing; there is only a discourse which, in its entirety, can be called 'literary'.

The insistence that the author's traditional and previously unquestioned authority over the critic is finished is a constant feature of post-war literary criticism. Again and again, the death knell is sounded for any distinction between 'creative' writing and 'critical' writing: an antithesis that far from incidentally provides the entire narrative momentum for *The Paper Men*. In his book *Literary Theory: An Introduction* (Oxford, 1983), Terry Eagleton briefly, and perhaps mercifully, summarizes the relevant aspects of the literary approach known as deconstruction:

> All language, for Derrida, displays this 'surplus' over exact meaning, is always threatening to outrun and escape the sense which tries to contain it. 'Literary' discourse is the place where this is most evident, but it is also true of all other writing; deconstruction rejects the literary/ non-literary opposition as any absolute distinction. (p. 134)

By no means all literary critics, and even fewer novelists, are sympathetic to the implications of such theories, and readers of *The Paper Men* all too readily assume that Wilf Barclay, and therefore William Golding, would be among those who are hostile. But *The Paper Men* actually celebrates the death of the author, making it certainly Golding's wittiest and most audacious novel. In addition, the novel's consistently harmonious integration of two distinct narrative levels provides another reason for considering *The Paper Men* as among Golding's best books, not one of his worst.

The Paper Men, like *Darkness Visible*, consistently invites the reader to evaluate every incident metaphorically. Even the most unsympathetic reader of Barthes's 'The Death of the Author', for example, must admit that the essay exists, for better or worse, as an historical fact. In 1968, while students violently questioned the traditional authority of their elders on the streets of Paris, Barthes's essay questioned the traditional *author*ity of the author. Golding presents a cunningly buried commentary on the crumbling role of fictional authority in *The Paper Men*, when he has the American Tucker mocking English Wilf Barclay, by using an event which can be similarly verified by history:

> You were going on about the British social system ... You gave examples of their perfect devotion, like traditional conservative civil servants organizing the nationalization of industry for the socialists. Only of course ... we'd just heard the way your civil service was full of Philby and those guys. Laugh? People were falling about.

Until the time of the Philby, Burgess, Maclean scandal, although manifestly no longer a world power, England was still deferred to in the field of espionage by an inestimably stronger America, as is implied in books such as Andrew Boyle's *The Climate of Treason* and Chapman Pincher's *Too Secret Too Long*. This deference was freely given, principally because England's authoritative attitude, created by centuries of experience in the Great Game, assumed it as a right. The incident that Tucker refers to above is the historical moment that this traditional deference to England's authority in matters of espionage died, and it is used in Golding's novel to parallel the collapse of the critic's traditional deference to the authority of the creative artist.

Throughout the novel, Rick Tucker is seen to be a great teller of tales, in fact a liar; while Wilf Barclay constantly denies invention in favour of selecting and adjusting incidents from 'real' life. The two men slowly adopt one another's roles and it is significant that Tucker eventually kills Barclay (the death of the author) for writing his own biography instead of allowing the critic to do it. This denial of an apparent opposition is paralleled as Barclay undergoes two very different experiences: the first a violent, horrifying experience in the cathedral on the island of Lipari; and the other a joyous, beatific vision on the Spanish Steps in Rome. Although these incidents seem to be visions of Hell and Heaven respectively, *The Paper Men* concludes with the suggestion that both visions are in reality One; that without the horror of Lipari there could be no joyous vision in Rome. The literary denial of distinctions is accompanied by a spiritual denial of distinctions, and the concepts of literary authority and spiritual authority interact throughout the novel.

The declining authority of both art and the artist is a central theme of the novel, and it is significant that, in the opening pages Barclay describes his wife in imagery taken from television: 'Then, as if she had switched channels, she became the perfect hostess.' Near the end of the novel, Johnny informs Barclay that he is no longer a writer but is now a TV celebrity. The crumbling authority of the written word is then immediately emphasized as the reader is returned to the espionage incident referred to above, because for no apparent reason other than that of directing the reader's attention back to the Philby incident, Johnny's show is called *I Spy*. Various other media, particularly film, are used in the novel to query the traditional assumption of superiority claimed by the printed word. When Tucker takes a photograph of his wife with Barclay, the incident economically demonstrates Barclay's immediate response to the beauty of Mary Lou, and also provides a further observation on the relationship that exists between art and reality: 'The camera cannot have caught her warmth and softness. It was what you might call a close encounter of the second kind, no image of a girl but the pliant, perfumed, actual.' Within this statement there is a covert reference to Steven Spielberg's *Close Encounters of the Third Kind*, one of the most successful films ever made. Golding's use here of two such contemporary art forms as photography and film reinforces the suggestion that, in the late twentieth century, the author is dead in more ways than one.

Golding suggests in *The Paper Men* that precisely because the majority of people prefer to watch television rather than involve themselves in art, a subtle theological inference has attached itself to art and the artist. Art has replaced religion in contemporary intellectual life. It is now art that possesses 'meaning' and 'significance', and it is the function of the critic in particular to find this 'meaning'. This assumption places the author in a position of God-like authority over his own work. The author alone knows its true meaning, and naturally literary criticism, which seeks to discover this ultimate authoritative message, functions within so secular an environment as a form of contemporary theology.

Wittily, this novel, in which Barclay deplores the concept of literary originality being assessed in a way that is so unflattering to the author's vanity, is itself structured upon a literary text, Marlowe's *Doctor Faustus*. Any reader of *The Paper Men* who has even a rudimentary knowledge of Golding's other work will be aware that many of his novels are based on other literary texts. Although Golding's extensive use of other literary works is usually subversive, and he exposes the failures of the older text in the novel into which he has integrated it, this is, importantly, not what he has done in *The Paper Men*. This novel's use of Marlowe's *Doctor Faustus* shares with *Free Fall*'s incorporation of Dante's *La Vita Nuova* its use of the backgrounded text as an exemplary model. In each case, the world depicted in Golding's novel becomes paltry when it is compared with the world view of the original work. *Doctor Faustus* portrays a world in which damnation is at least possible, a world of enormous spiritual power. Barclay's experiences in *The Paper Men*, suggest that, compared to the world of *Doctor Faustus*, the spiritually impoverished contemporary world is bleak and shallow. Golding's use of *Doctor Faustus* serves to emphasize the way in which contemporary society sees art as a substitute for the spiritual. Mephistopheles, for example, originally played a symbolic role as Evil in a specifically religious discourse, but he is also a literary archetype. This is how he is used in *The Paper Men*; as one whose resonance for the majority of people is considerably more structured in the literary than it is in the religious, and the novel queries this shift.

While *The Paper Men* repudiates the assumption that writers are possessed of oracular powers, it implies that the imperfection of the gospel is not due to the depravity and unworthiness of the author as a person. *The Paper Men* further rejects the belief that art can provide an alternative meaning to life in the absence of spiritual truth, and suggests that only the spiritual reality at the centre of life is of any importance. Barclay himself is persistently and uneasily aware that there is nothing profound about his own life; instead, he recognizes that what hovers about him is the complete opposite: 'the spirit of farce'.

Throughout *The Paper Men*, Barclay constantly expresses the fear that his life could be reducible to farce, which he sees as inelegant and ridiculous. Barclay fears his life has lacked seriousness and significance, and he invariably comments upon his own past in images that are principally derived both from the genre of farce and from the circus: 'I didn't lose my trousers. I hadn't a round, red nose and ginger hair and a painted squint.' Through Tucker's probing, Barclay remembers taking an aphrodisiac which caused him to suffer a painful case of priapism in a sordidly comic incident that occurred during his youth while he was working in a bank. There seems little doubt that the graphic descriptions of Barclay's aching erection and fruitless masturbations are deliberately juxtaposed with references to T. S. Eliot, probably the most celebrated author this century to work in a bank, in order that the sense of gravitas, which the very name of Eliot evokes, will serve to emphasize the degrading and farcical elements of Barclay's behaviour. Barclay uses the incident to summarize the prevalent role of farce in his life:

> It was the spirit of farce, of course. In one way I could describe my whole life as a movement from one moment of farce to another, farce on one plane or another, nature's comic, her clown with a red nose, ginger hair and trousers falling down at precisely the wrong moment. Yes, right from the cradle. The first time I shot over a horse's head my fall was broken by a pile of dung.

This insistence upon reducing life into clearly distinguishable literary genres is a trait that Barclay shares with the protagonist of *Rites of Passage*, and, perhaps most importantly for the central issues of *The Paper Men*, this obsessional need to categorize and differentiate is a charge more commonly levelled at critics.

Initially, Barclay is as concerned that nobody should discover the farcical elements of his life as he is that nobody will uncover the more serious and even criminal actions he has committed; such as the Lucinda episode, the recovery of the letters, and the presumed killing of the Indian. It is, essentially, the principal reason he is opposed to a biography, and he squirms at the thought of his clownish behaviour being revealed for the world to see. There is obviously a certain amount of quite understandable vanity involved in his fear of being perceived as a comic character, but there is also a suggestion here that this preoccupation of Barclay's is an inevitable result of the overblown awe and reverence in which the artist is held.

There is a sense of meaninglessness in the life Barclay describes himself living after his separation from Liz. Entire years pass in an aimless blur of sodden travel, and it is quite clear that there is little joy in his drinking. It is significant that his travels become more directionless and frantic, while his drinking increases in intensity, after the literary conference in Seville, when he has read the papers from the conference. Despair descends on Barclay upon his realization that authors are now denied their traditional garments of authority and originality. His work is rendered meaningless to him, because others perceive in it only borrowings from other texts, and as he flees Tucker's clutches the distinction between fiction and reality is further blurred by his constant inebriation.

Golding's later fiction is striking for the way in which his characters dispense with traditional modes of enlightenment: the paths of duty, virtue and 'gentle Jesus meek and mild'. Golding's later fiction often depicts the attainment of truth through the sinful paths of 'outrage'. In *Darkness Visible*, Matty kills a fellow pupil, Pedigree is a paedophile, while Sophy has visions of murdering the kidnapped boy in cold blood. In *Rites of Passage*, Colley discovers, through alcohol, sodomy and fellatio, 'the horror, the horror' at the centre of life. Shame, sex, and alcohol animate *The Paper Men*, and while the lying, drunken Barclay dies in a state of spiritual serenity, his innocent wife dies of cancer. There is a biblical, Old Testament, harshness and austerity about this cancer which is quite consistent with the novel's concerns. Like the two novels that immediately precede it, *The Paper Men* is not concerned with concepts such as fairness and justice, but with the irrational, numinous force which is at the centre of life, and which can be apprehended as much, if not more, by outrage, as it can by conventional piety. In this respect all three novels dramatize William Blake's famous assertion: 'The paths of excess lead to the palaces of wisdom.'

In 1980 Golding published *Rites of Passage*, which won the prestigious Booker Prize. This novel, with *Lord of the Flies* his most widely read and popular book, is the first instalment in what was to become a trilogy. Just as *Free Fall* can be read as a *Künstlerroman*, *Rites of Passage* can be seen as *Bildungsroman*, a novel of general education. The first person narrative recounts the adventures of Edmund Talbot, a well-educated young man of the upper classes who is on a ship bound for Australia in 1812–13, during a lull in the Napoleonic wars. Talbot begins the book as a snobbish, arrogant, and vain representative of the upper classes, but becomes a more thoughtful and compassionate man as the journey progresses. The person who brings about this change in Talbot is Colley, a young clergyman from a lower social class. During the voyage, Colley gets drunk and after making a general fool of himself takes to his bed, apparently too embarrassed to appear in public. However, three days later, having refused all food and drink, he dies. *Rites of Passage* is constructed as a journal, and within Talbot's journal the reader is offered Colley's journal; a technique which allows Golding to use two first person narratives. The reader, along with Talbot, eventually learns that Colley had done more when drunk than simply make a fool of himself; he had performed fellatio on a sailor and had been sodomized by an unspecified number of the crew. The shame of this, so Talbot believes, is what killed Colley.

Rites of Passage, like so much of Golding's earlier fiction, is indebted to an earlier source; in this case Elizabeth Longford's *Life of Wellington* (vol. 1, London, 1969):

> After only three days at sea the unfortunate clergyman got 'abominably' drunk and rushed out of his cabin stark naked among the soldiers and sailors 'talking all sorts of bawdy and ribaldry and singing scraps of the most blackguard and indecent songs'. Such was his shame on afterwards hearing of these 'irregularities' that he shut himself up and refused to eat or speak ... In ten days he forced himself to die of contrition. (p. 51)

It is possible that it was not only the actual death of the parson that prompted Golding to write *Rites of Passage,* but also the baldness and lack of detail in the account. There is an austerity about it which is quite horrifying, and to invent the 'human circumstances' of an event is paradoxically to make it more *real.*

However, the assumption, in the last sentence quoted above, that the author somehow 'knows' that the clergyman 'forced himself to die of contrition' is interesting. How does the author know? How can any of us ever know what another human being is experiencing? Even if we could know, how could we communicate our knowledge? It is these questions which *Rites of Passage* attempts to answer. The novel is structured around the related activities of reading and writing, and in addition there are numerous references to painting and to the theatre. Even this array of artistic modes is, individually or collectively, unable to explain Colley's mysterious and lonely death. *Rites of Passage,* one of Golding's most polished and articulate novels, paradoxically describes the inability of art, any art, adequately to represent reality. This preoccupation is also found in *The Paper Men,* and Wilf Barclay actually shouts 'Words are useless'.

Shame can be seen as a public experience, and *Rites of Passage* is clearly concerned with social class. Talbot and Colley are reminiscent of Bobby and Oliver in *The Pyramid,* but Golding also uses the aristocrat and the parson to represent different forces within another crucial moment in history. With its use of the dual narrative perspective, *Rites of Passage* can be viewed as a novel which is structured around the conflict between Augustanism and Romanticism. Talbot's elegant, learned, and affected prose style shows him as an Augustan, a Neo-Classicist, the literary heir of Lord Chesterfield, Dryden, and Pope. The vibrant, spiritual energy of Colley's prose conversely reveals him as a Romantic, heir to a radical new poetic vision – that of Coleridge, Keats, and Byron. By the novel's conclusion, Talbot has learned enough to see that, irrespective of class, Colley was a highly gifted writer, and his own prose style becomes more flexible as a result. This stylistic development in Talbot is paralleled by a comparable moral development.

The first lieutenant, Summers, is a good officer who has made his way through the ranks. Although Talbot consequently dismisses Summers, preferring the better bred Deverel, it is the first lieutenant's insistence that it is Talbot's duty to visit the sick man which forces Talbot to recognize that he is not a spectator in a theatre, but a participant in a real life and death. Talbot begins to accept the reality of other lives, distinct from their entertainment value to himself, and, indeed, inseparably connected to his own actions. Although Summers teaches Talbot the value of masculine friendship throughout the trilogy, each one of the three novels focuses upon a character who teaches Talbot the most valuable lesson he will learn within that particular novel. In *Rites of Passage* it is Colley who obliquely informs Talbot of an irrational dimension to human experience which Talbot had not even dreamt existed, and his influence affects Talbot's form of expression. In *Fire Down Below* Mr Prettiman is Talbot's tutor in politics, and his influence is profound; but in *Close Quarters* the beautiful Miss Chumley is Talbot's tutor in the emotional life, and her lessons extend into Talbot's understanding of art.

Close Quarters has an even more straightforward story line than *Rites of Passage*. It describes Talbot's further adventures, the most important of which is his meeting with Miss Chumley, a passenger aboard *Alcyone*, which Talbot's ship encounters in mid-ocean. Miss Chumley very effectively furthers Talbot's education by causing him to fall deeply and passionately in love with her. In fact, he is so smitten he suffers a breakdown. The dashing and flamboyant Lieutenant Benét also transfers to Talbot's ship, and his rivalry with Summers provides the most interesting conflict within the novel. While Benét represents flair and boldness, Summers represents competence and caution, and their differing outlooks on how best to sail the ship clash throughout the novel.

This second volume also develops Talbot's preoccupation with 'Tarpaulin', the highly specialized vocabulary of the sailors, which he had begun savouring and collecting from the opening pages of *Rites of Passage*. As the title implies, this second novel has a more claustrophobic atmosphere than its predecessor, and, as the world begins to shrink to the confines of the ship, the sailors' language gradually dominates ordinary social discourse. The novel's concerns are specifically focused and it is structured around a few key incidents. Perhaps the most important of these is the 'dragrope incident' near the end of the novel, when the sailors attempt to clean the underside of the ship, a scene which Talbot recounts in fluent Tarpaulin. The extensive presentation of Tarpaulin within *Close Quarters* involves the depiction of it both as a structural entity, and also as a vehicle for continuing Talbot's moral education. In Talbot's relationships with Miss Chumley and with the ship's officers, Summers in particular, *Close Quarters* is a novel of overcompensation, of excess: mistakes Talbot makes in *Rites of Passage* are rectified without moderation, resulting in further mistakes within *Close Quarters*. In *Close Quarters*, Talbot's feelings for Miss Chumley so massively overcompensate for the purely carnal desire which he displays towards Zenobia in *Rites of Passage*, that he resolutely refuses even to contemplate her sexually. A similarly excessive reaction to an earlier misdemeanour is detectable in Talbot's dealings with the ship's officers. Talbot begins *Rites of Passage* by assuming that Deverel is a better officer than Summers, which he is not, because he is a gentleman, which he is. Although Talbot eventually admits his mistake, his relationships with the ship's officers, until the virtual conclusion of *Close Quarters*, display his arrogant attitude toward their trade.

Like many well-educated people, Talbot is slow to value practical skills, or to respect sufficiently the considerable intelligence that is required to interact with, and to control, the physical universe. In *Rites of Passage*, Talbot is civil to Summers and wary of Captain Anderson; only belatedly, in *Close Quarters*, does he recognize that their technical proficiency is genuine ability of a completely different nature from his own. This comprehension, like his realization that there are finer feelings for a woman than the purely sexual, also involves the reversal of an earlier, erroneous attitude first displayed in *Rites of Passage*. Similarly, it also involves excess and overcompensation, and although Talbot's attitude towards the officers is ostensibly quite different from his attitude to Miss Chumley, they are, fundamentally, identical.

Talbot's excessive reaction to earlier errors results, firstly, in his perception of Miss Chumley solely as the apotheosis of ethereal beauty and, secondly, in his perception of the officers solely as superbly useful exemplars of technical ability. Essentially, therefore, Talbot turns the officers into machines and Miss Chumley into a goddess, and consequently denies all of them their individual humanity. The powerful human emotions which are depicted during the dragrope episode are of crucial importance in suggesting possible redress for the excessively restrictive perception of the officers that Talbot has adopted.

Talbot translates Summers's practical ability into a vision of steely masculinity, and subsequently he cannot credit the officer with emotions that are at variance with this ideal. When speaking of the relationships between the officers with Mr Jones, Talbot will not say the word 'jealous', as 'it would seem to credit Charles Summers with an almost feminine weakness'. Similarly, when Talbot overhears an exchange between Benét and the Captain, he says of it: 'Good God – but this was *arch*!' Talbot's emphasis may imply disgust, or surprise, or amusement; but its very presence indicates that it is a criticism of the ideal image that in his excessive zeal he has constructed of the two officers. He is blind to the fact that everybody, even the most fluent speaker of Tarpaulin, shares a common humanity.

Talbot still has an important lesson in human nature left to learn before the conclusion of *Close Quarters*, and it is prepared for in the dragrope incident. During the *rapprochement* of Talbot and Summers there can be few readers who are not simultaneously moved and amused by Summers's characteristically Tarpaulin expressions, even when he is discussing his emotions: 'Yet my attachments are deep and strong. Men, like cables, have each their breaking strain.' This deftly presented scene fulfils several functions, and it is perhaps of particular significance that the misunderstanding between the two men is the fault of Summers, which strengthens his autonomous existence as a character by distancing him from the role of moral exemplar. It is noticeable, too, that Talbot's defence requires him to consult his journal; a final reference to the importance of reading which is so pervasive a feature of both *Rites of Passage* and *Close Quarters*. Perhaps most importantly of all for Talbot, Summers forces him to realize that masculinity and emotion are not mutually exclusive. The incident functions overall as a summary of Talbot's moral education to date, and the reader does not doubt Talbot's sincerity when he says to Summers: 'Measured against you I am a paltry fellow, that is the fact of the matter!' The relationship between the two men is also central to *Fire Down Below* and, as in the earlier two novels, Talbot's liking for Summers is commented upon by other characters to imply that Talbot has grown into a better man.

Throughout the three novels, the development in Talbot's moral perspective is perhaps the most striking of all the changes he experiences. The youthful intensity of his cynicism and ambition are both considerably diminished by the conclusion of *Fire Down Below.* In *Close Quarters* he sacrifices his ambition for Miss Chumley, 'All for Love', heedless of her poverty, and in *Fire Down Below* she repays this considerable compliment by agreeing to marry him before his prospects are revived. When Talbot's cynical and exploitative treatment of Zenobia is contrasted with his feelings for Miss Chumley, it will be seen that one of Talbot's very great accomplishments within the trilogy is to fall in love. Not only do Talbot's values change, but he also develops sufficiently to feel remorse for attitudes he once blithely believed to be his birthright. By the conclusion of the voyage, Talbot is considerably less aristocratic in his assumptions than he was at the start of *Rites of Passage.* A brief, but highly significant, example of this is suggested when he is informed by Mr Bowles that Mr Prettiman is very much respected by the seamen and emigrants, to which Talbot replies: 'Have I dismissed him as a clown too readily?'

Fire Down Below brings the trilogy to its conclusion. The *Britannia* lands safely in Australia, only to be destroyed by fire. Talbot encounters Miss Chumley again and she accepts his proposal of marriage. Talbot will return to England and become a prosperous, public man, one who talks regularly with the Prime Minister. It seems like a happy ending – but in this, his last novel, Golding implies that appearances can be deceptive.

Inevitably, *Fire Down Below* shares many of the same interests as *Rites of Passage* and *Close Quarters.* Because Talbot is leaving the sea, Tarpaulin, again inevitably, recedes as an issue, so that when the ship docks in Australia Talbot makes a clear distinction between Tarpaulin and his own language. His general interest in language, however, remains constant, and the *power* of language also remains a strong theme within *Fire Down Below.*

The details of Benét's ingenious engineering, and the overall description of life at sea, are convincingly realistic. This realism, however, is then subverted by an emphasis on fictionality and artificiality. Talbot's comment on the condition of the convicts who have been transported to Australia, for example, is unequivocally anachronistic: 'These fellows have found this shore in no way fatal to them!' This is a clear reference to *The Fatal Shore*, Robert Hughes's highly acclaimed account of the transportation of convicts to Australia, a book which was published in 1987, two years before the publication of *Fire Down Below*. The quite deliberate nature of his anachronistic reference subverts the purposive historical authenticity of Talbot's writing and draws attention to the fictionality of the novel. Golding adds yet another element of artificiality to *Fire Down Below* by imparting a characteristic of his own to one of the characters in the novel. In *Golding* (Edinburgh, 1969) Leighton Hodson refers to an incident which occurred during Golding's war service: 'On one occasion a nervous tic, produced by stress and hazard, twisted his face into what appeared to be a wide grin of bloodthirsty elation. As the danger increased the grin grew even wider' (p.11). It can hardly be a coincidence, therefore, that when the wall of ice appears in *Fire Down Below*, Talbot's description of Captain Anderson's reaction is strikingly similar to the account of Golding's own behaviour: 'He looked at me and smiled that same ghastly smile which he occasionally inflicted on persons near him at moments of extreme danger.' Innumerable circumstances conspire to convince the reader that nothing is necessarily as it appears. There are the many references to 'truth being stranger than fiction', as well as the conclusion of the novel itself, which even Talbot refers to as 'fairy tale'.

Throughout the trilogy, one of Golding's most characteristic narrative devices is the plausible delay of significant information. In *Rites of Passage*, Talbot does not read Colley's journal until the novel is almost over, while in *Close Quarters*, Wheeler does not pass on Miss Chumley's note until almost the same point has been reached. In *Fire Down Below*, this same principle of narrative delay ensures that Benét's origins are not revealed until the ship has docked in Australia, and then Benét and Summers can be seen as representing another dichotomy; this time they function respectively as representatives of the Revolutionary temperament of France, and the more conservative, politically phlegmatic attitude of the English.

As always, this is plausibly done. Miss Chumley, naturally, had come to know Benét aboard the *Alcyone*, and it is she who tells Talbot that Benét's father 'started the French Revolution' and that as a result the family had to flee France. The reader, of course, has to wonder if this is what Benét actually said, for he is not above a little exaggeration if it might impress an attractive young woman, or if this is Miss Chumley's interpretation of what he said. In any event, Benét's boldness, although attractive, seems to result in the destruction of the ship, while the cautious Summers dies in a doomed attempt to put out the fire. Politically, the novel is similar to *The Brass Butterfly*, where change is seen as invariably disastrous. However, there are ambiguities here. After all, Benét's plan did get the ship to Australia, and it is also implied that fireworks, not Benét's engineering, causes the blaze.

While *Rites of Passage* dwells on Talbot's spiritual development, and *Close Quarters* focuses on Miss Chumley's lessons in love and poetry, *Fire Down Below* begins Talbot's political education, and his teacher is Mr Prettiman. Talbot is, momentarily, blinded by Mr Prettiman's political vision, and he writes rhapsodically about his new understanding: 'I had even glimpsed, or thought I glimpsed, our universe as a bubble afloat in the incommensurable golden sea of the Absolute, the myriad sparks of fire, each the jewel in the head of an animal which could "look up".' But Talbot cannot accompany the Prettimans to 'Eldorado'. He will not give up the world. Talbot is like Oliver in *The Pyramid* and will never pay more than a fair price. *Fire Down Below* is written as an autobiography and in its final pages there is a sadness which undermines all the references to 'happy endings'. Talbot has had a good life, but he still dreams of 'Eldorado' and the path he was temperamentally unable to take. 'Everything costs' could serve not only as an epigraph to *Fire Down Below* but to virtually everything Golding wrote. In his last novel, as he had done throughout all his writings, Golding contrasts the rational with the spiritual, and echoes of the spiritual resonate throughout the closing pages of the novel, haunting Talbot with visions of what he has lost.

4

The Double Tongue (1995)

... haunting Talbot with visions of what he has lost.

Golding died in 1993, but in 1995 Faber published the manuscript he was working on at the time of his death as *The Double Tongue*. Bearing in mind that this is only a second draft, *The Double Tongue* is a remarkable book, and no doubt, had its author lived longer, it would have been even more remarkable. As the protagonist and narrator of *The Double Tongue*, Arieka, muses on the ambivalence of the Oracle's responses to her questions, she notes: 'There was always something in the answer which could be interpreted in different ways.' *The Double Tongue*, too, can be interpreted in different ways. Like *The Inheritors, The Spire, The Pyramid, The Scorpion God, Rites of Passage, Close Quarters* and *Fire Down Below*, the book is another of Golding's historical novels, this time set in Greece in the first century BC. Now an elderly woman, Arieka surveys her life in terms of the utmost equivocation. A plain girl, with little chance of securing a husband, and further burdened with purported psychic powers, about which she was then, and is still now, herself sceptical, she is in effect sold to Ionides, the hereditary priest of Apollo. Ionides is gay, cynical and charming; he needs a biddable mouthpiece, a 'Pythia' for Apollo's answers at Delphi's omniscient Oracle. Although at the outset of the novel Arieka is the number three oracle, the two senior oracles almost immediately die and it is Arieka who must go down into Apollo's cave and transmit the words of the god. However, whether this is what she actually does is an issue at the centre of *The Double Tongue*. Is it really the god speaking? Or is it Arieka herself? As indeed the book's title suggests, *The Double Tongue* centres around doubt, scepticism and equivocation. Like Golding's earlier historical fictions, *The Double Tongue* uses its setting to raise issues that transcend the temporality of its chronological siting.

The book received mixed reviews, and a number of them were dismissive, suggesting that, at best, it was of primarily biographical interest. However, *The Double Tongue* has several structural and thematic similarities with many of Golding's earlier books. Its striking opening sentence, for example: 'Blazing light and warmth, undifferentiated and experiencing themselves' raises the same epistemological issues as does the orgasm Sophy experiences in *Darkness Visible*: 'then for a timeless time where was no Sophy. No *this*. Nothing but release, existing, impossibly by itself.' Arieka continues: 'No words, no time, not even I, ego, since as I tried to say, the warmth and blazing light was experiencing itself, if you see what I mean.' Similarly, the retrospective form of the narrative and its subsequent, and inevitable, preoccupation with memory, links it firmly with *Free Fall*. In one of her numerous discussions with Ionides, Arieka informs him, 'I've been reading about the oracle. This time it was about the legend and saying that the Old Religion was woman's.' This conception of a religion which is female is at the centre of Lok's people's view of the universe in *The Inheritors*, while the curt manner in which Ionides dismisses the librarian, Perseus, evokes Wilf Barclay's brutal rejection of literary criticism in *The Paper Men*: 'Go back to your books about books about books. We'll be content with the makers.' *The Spire* is also evoked in *The Double Tongue*, when Arieka is forced to become acquainted with the terminology of builders, masons and carpenters as the buildings in which the oracle's servants live become dangerously unsound, requiring, of course, a great deal of money to remedy the damage. Even more strikingly, however, *The Double Tongue* shares a fascination with the representation and terminology of theatre in *Rites of Passage*.

Talbot sees a stage in any setting and is quite oblivious to the incongruity: 'We were spectators and there, interruptedly, seen beyond the boats on the boom and the huge cylinder of the mainmast, was the stage.' Talbot is, of course, very much mistaken when he jocularly begins suggesting genres which would be applicable to describe Colley's actions:

> It is a play. Is it a farce or a tragedy? Does not a tragedy depend on the dignity of the protagonist? Must he not be great to fall greatly? A farce, then, for the man appears now a sort of Punchinello. His fall is in social terms. Death does not come into it.

Death does come into it. By mistaking life for art, Talbot denies Colley's humanity. The hint of Aristotelian pedantry in Talbot's definition of tragedy, and its patent unsuitability in connection with any person's actual death, is contrasted with the real agony of Colley. Eventually, however, one of the many lessons that Talbot learns in the course of the voyage is precisely that art is not life: 'I was never made so aware of the distance between the disorder of real life in all its multifarious action, partial exhibition, irritating concealments and the stage simulacra that I had once taken as a fair representation of it.' In *The Double Tongue*, however, while theatrical imagery abounds, it is never made clear whether the language of theatre is appropriate to describe the events – or quite inappropriate. Such ambivalence and equivocation is at the heart of this novel. Arieka is much perturbed by the possibility that, rather than being a Pythia and a high priest, she and Ionides are really actress and stage manager:

> And we? We moderns? We had made a play of it, with scenery and a cast, with triviality, so that it became much as its new surrounds were. All that glitters was gold, except the words. I had spoken words and not known I had spoken them. They were the god's words.
>
> Except those spoken by Ionides.

The 'except' here is characteristic of the novel. Is it the god who speaks? Or is it Ionides? Nothing is ever made clear.

From the outset of the novel, ambiguity is privileged. As a child, Arieka realizes 'The god speaks with a double tongue,' while later she speculates on her own embryonic ability: 'It is a furtive power ... furtive and dishonest, knows how to hide, how to claim, how to disguise, avoid, speak double like the snake or not at all.' Later, when a Pythia, she links herself, Ionides and the oracle: 'I began to see how the oracle, like Ionides, was surrounded by contradictions.' Both Ionides and Arieka herself are riven by contradictions, inconsistencies and equivocations: 'So Ionides, cynic, atheist, contriver, liar, believed in God!' It is possible that the god exists, and it is equally possible that he does not.

Several reviewers complained that *The Double Tongue* was lacking in detail, with some suggesting that Golding might well have added more details to some of the more skeletal scenes in later drafts. Equally, however, it is possible to suggest that in *The Double Tongue*, as never before, Golding is interested in essences, and so he consistently refuses to allow the traditional trappings of the realistic mode to impede the progress of his elegant and provocative fable.

The Double Tongue is a fable preoccupied with the ambivalence at the heart of existence, an ontological concern which links the book very firmly to *The Paper Men*. Similarly, when Arieka speaks contemptuously of dreams – 'Everyday we rid ourselves of the rubbish of our bodies. I think that in sleep with its dreams we are trying to rid ourselves of the rubbish of our minds' – the reader may recall the sweeping dismissal in Golding's essay 'Belief and Creativity' quoted earlier: 'Marx, Darwin and Freud are the three most crashing bores of the Western world.' Neither of these comments is simple iconoclasm, and in Arieka's case Golding implies that the power she senses is not to be found within her 'subconscious' but, if it exists at all, lies outside herself, at the centre of existence itself.

The Double Tongue is deftly and economically written, with a wry humour present throughout. There are, as might be expected in a Golding novel, some magnificent set-pieces, among the most powerful of which are the description of Arieka's first descent into the cave of Apollo, and her youthful belief that the gods of her childhood have abandoned her:

> Anyway, in that small room, with its pallet, its single chest, its hooks with one or two cloaks hanging from them, there in the artificial twilight she dropped down into grief, into sorrow before the shame. She dissolved away like a lump of salt in fresh water. There was nothing but grief before the retreating backs of the gods: then they were gone.

The Double Tongue is a meditation on doubt, a celebration of uncertainty. The narrator, a woman in her eighties, just as Golding was a man in his eighties when he wrote the book, is never sure if she really was an interpreter of the great mysteries, or simply a mere entertainer. It is not at all implausible to suggest that, in *The Double Tongue*, Golding offers us an oblique commentary on the artist's vocation, and, more specifically, on his own. In his final novel, Golding poses a question which he does not himself answer: do artists have access to a deeper wisdom, do they possess a profundity of vision, itself lying outside their own comprehension – or are they charlatans, dazzling their audience with what amounts to little more than technical expertise and manipulative trickery? Given the size of Golding's contribution to the English novel, *The Double Tongue* is a remarkably modest, even humble, novel – and a valuable addition to an extraordinary legacy.

William Golding extended the formal boundaries of fiction and made a significant contribution to England's literature. In the famous preface to his story *The Nigger of the 'Narcissus'*, Joseph Conrad wrote that his job was, above all, to make his readers *'see'*. In its extraordinary control and ingenious use of narrative perspective Golding's work also made his readers *'see'*. Like an earlier literary innovator, T. S. Eliot, Golding returned to the past in search of the stories that still reverberate through our culture, which he then used to create myths for a modern age. Golding's characters are rarely helpless victims of socio-economic forces beyond their control. They live in a world where tragedy is not just present, but actively inscribed in the nature of things, a world in which one must choose and where the consequences of the wrong choice can be fatal. Golding's mythic and allegorical universe is one where damnation and salvation are still possible and where the actions of a single individual have an effect on the world. For all its tragedy and pessimism, therefore, it can be seen as a world that has meaning; one which affirms and celebrates the unique humanity of every individual.

Select Bibliography

WORKS BY WILLIAM GOLDING

These titles are listed in chronological order and, with the exception of *Poems*, are all published by Faber and Faber, London.

Poems (London: Macmillan's Contemporary Poets, 1934)
Lord of the Flies (1954)
The Inheritors (1955)
Pincher Martin (1956)
The Brass Butterfly (1958)
Free Fall (1959)
The Spire (1964)
The Hot Gates (1965)
The Pyramid (1967)
The Scorpion God (1971)
Darkness Visible (1979)
Rites of Passage (1980)
A Moving Target (1982)
The Paper Men (1984)
An Egyptian Journal (1985)
Close Quarters (1987)
Fire Down Below (1989)
The Double Tongue (1995)

BIBLIOGRAPHY

Gekoski, R. A., and P. A. Grogan, *William Golding: A Bibliography* (London: André Deutsch, 1994). A comprehensive, deluxe, limited edition.

BIOGRAPHICAL AND CRITICAL STUDIES

There has, as of 2004, been no biography of William Golding, nor is there any published correspondence.

Babb, Howard, *The Novels of William Golding* (Ohio: Ohio State University Press, 1970). A well-documented and persuasively argued book.

Baker, James, *William Golding: A Critical Study* (New York: St Martin's Press, 1965). A comprehensive early study, concluding with an assessment of *The Spire*.

Baker, James (ed.), *Critical Essays on William Golding* (Boston: G. K. Hall & Co., 1988). A wide-ranging collection of essays from a number of well-known Golding critics which evaluates all of Golding's novels up to the date of publication.

Biles, Jack, *Talk: Conversation with William Golding* (New York: Harcourt Brace Jovanovich, 1970). Illuminating discussions with Golding that cover Golding's childhood reading, his interest in Greek literature and his fascination with myth and fable. In a similar vein see John Haffenden, *Novelists In Interview*.

Bloom, Harold (ed.), *William Golding's Lord of the Flies* (Philadelphia, PA: Chelsea House, 1999). An extremely comprehensive collection of essays on *Lord of the Flies* from some of the world's leading Golding scholars, prefaced with an illuminating introduction by Harold Bloom.

Boyd, S. J., *The Novels of William Golding* (Sussex: Harvester Press, 1988; subsequently revised to include an evaluation of *Fire Down Below*). Focuses on the moral aspects of Golding's novels and attempts to place the author within the English literary tradition.

Carey, John (ed.), *William Golding, The Man and His Books: A Tribute on his 75th Birthday* (London: Faber, 1986). A collection of essays by a number of writers and critics which mixes interesting biographical information, personal reminiscences and traditional criticism.

Crompton, Don, *A View From The Spire: William Golding's Later Novels* (Oxford, Blackwell, 1985). An acute and discriminating evaluation of the novels Golding published between 1964 and 1984.

Dick, Bernard, *William Golding* (New York: Twayne Publishers, 1967; revised in 1987). A useful assessment of all Golding's work up to the date of revision.

Dicken-Fuller, Nicola, *William Golding's Use Of Symbolism* (Sussex: The Book Guild, 1990). A book which briefly considers all of Golding's fiction and is written in a very accessible manner, but which is necessarily restricted by its focus on symbolism.

Dickson, L. L., *The Modern Allegories of William Golding* (Florida: University of South Florida Press, 1990). Quite comprehensive, but not as tightly focused as its title may suggest.

Friedman, Lawrence, *William Golding* (New York: Continuum, 1993). A brief and lucid survey which integrates Golding's life with his work.

Gindin, James, *William Golding* (London: Macmillan 1988). A short book which covers all of Golding's novels up to the date of publication, and attempts to see Golding within a larger literary tradition.

Haffenden, John, *Novelists In Interview* (London: Methuen, 1985). Contains an interview with Golding, during which he talks mainly about *Rites of Passage*.

Hodson, Leighton, *Golding* (Edinburgh: Oliver and Boyd, 1969; revised to include an evaluation of *The Pyramid*). An early critical text which uses what little biographical information was available to trace the development of Golding's ideas.

Johnston, Arnold, *Of Earth and Darkness: The Novels of William Golding* (Missouri: University of Missouri Press, 1980). Covers all of Golding's fiction up to *Darkness Visible*, and offers an assessment of Golding's technical virtuosity.

Kinkead-Weekes, Mark and Ian Gregor, *William Golding: A Critical Study* (London: Faber and Faber, 1967; revised in 1984). An excellent and accessible book, still probably the best introduction to Golding's fiction.

Nelson, William (ed.), *William Golding's Lord of the Flies: A Source Book* (New York: The Odyssey Press, 1963). Despite its title it contains essays by a number of critics which cover all of Golding's fiction up to the date of publication. In addition it contains supplementary extracts from the work of philosophers such as Hobbes and Rousseau which allow the reader to place Golding's fiction against influential theories on humanity's relationship with evil.

Oldsey, Bernard S. and Stanley Weintraub, *The Art of William Golding* (Indiana: Indiana University Press, 1965). An early study, with a particular interest in technique, of all the fiction up to the date of publication.

Page, Norman (ed.), *William Golding: Novels, 1954–67* (London: Macmillan, 1987). A collection of essays which presents a selection of criticism of Golding's fiction up to and including *The Pyramid*. General surveys of his work are followed by individual studies of specific novels.

Redpath, Philip, *William Golding: A Structural Reading Of His Fiction* (London: Vision and Barnes and Noble, 1986). A somewhat undervalued book, this is a highly theoretical and most impressive reading of Golding's work which uses structuralist principles and employs challenging techniques for evaluation taken from contemporary literary theory.

Regard, Frédéric (ed.), *Fingering Netsukes: Selected Papers from the First International William Golding Conference* (Saint-Étienne: Publications de l'Université de Saint-Étienne, 1995). Published in association with Faber and Faber, this collection features essays on all aspects of Golding's work by a range of international authorities on Golding.

Subbarao, V. W., *William Golding: A Study* (London: Oriental Academic Press, 1987). A book by an Indian scholar which considers all of Golding's fiction up to *The Paper Men*.

Swisher, Clarice (ed.), *Readings on Lord of the Flies* (San Diego, CA: Greenhaven, 1997). Less demanding than the collection edited by Bloom, the book contains useful evaluations of Golding's first novel from a variety of perspectives.

Tiger, Virginia, *William Golding: The Dark Fields of Discovery* (London: Marion Boyars, 1974). One of the best of the earlier studies, with a heavy emphasis on the mythic dimensions of Golding's work and an equally convincing assessment of its structural complexity.

Index